TRAUMA QUEEN

A Broken Beauty Discovers God's Love

By
JULIE STAUTLAND

TABLE OF CONTENTS

DEDICATION

This book is dedicated to my dear husband, Tore,
who has been my pillar of strength, love,
and partner through life's journey.
You are my hero.

ACKNOWLEDGEMENTS

I will never be able to thank all the people who have impacted and blessed my life, but I will try my best to mention just a few.

To my parents, thank you for loving and supporting me despite how difficult your own situations were at times.

To my pastors and beloved friends, Matt and Lisa Tapley, thank you for living such an incredible example of 'running the race' for Christ despite all the trials that have come your way. The two of you have constantly poured out love onto others no matter what you were facing in your own lives.

To Barry and Sharon Slauenwhite, thank you for truly living out Christ's "Compassion". You have always been there for us, no matter what, even when it meant taking care of me for my last month of pregnancy with Mercedes.

To Rick and Diana Cua, what an example of God's grace and love you have been to me. Rick, even when I was suppose to take care of you on tour, you were watching out for me. And Diana, I can't thank you enough for the countless hours you imparted God's wisdom during my younger adult years.

To Bob and Carol Cave, thank you for living out your passion in missions and in your marriage with great selflessness and honesty.

To Tamara, our General Manager of TMG, and Andrew Preston, thank you for your invaluable friendship. Thank you, Tamara, for always going above and beyond with such dedication and commitment to work, family and friends.

To Dave and Shirley Kingston, thank you for all the years of friendship and help. You are some of the most dedicated workers for Christ that I know.

To Elea and David Harrison, thank you for being such great friends and neighbors. You have a wonderful gift of hospitality.

To Laura Lynn Tyler Thompson, thank you for your incredible enthusiasm and excitement for the message of restoration in Jesus.

To Todd and Niki Cantelon, Doug and Sandy McKenzie, Chris and Catharine Jones, Eric and Marcia Spath, Becky and John McNeil, John and Liz Hawley, Andrea and Mike Batts, Chris and Larry Neese, and Laura Lankin, and to all others I have forgotten, thank you for all the years of friendship and support.

To my beloved children, Mercedes and Trinity, I thank you for bringing such profound joy into my life everyday. It has been a privilege to be your mother and teacher.

And most importantly, to my beloved husband, thank you is not enough for all your love and support. You always believe in me. Life is a wonderful adventure with you. I am so thankful for your leadership and vision for whatever God places in front of you.

Endorsements

"Sharon and I have known Julie for some 25 years and we have come to love and admire her tenacity, generosity and godliness. She is a walking testimony of God's grace and faithfulness. "TRAUMA QUEEN – A Broken Beauty Discovers God's Love" will take you on a journey that may surprise you but one that we are sure will touch a common thread of most families. Be prepared to weep, smile and be amazed at God's power to overcome obstacles."

Dr. Barry & Sharon Slauenwhite
President & CEO
Compassion Canada

"Julie Stautland tells a profoundly gut-level honest story about the truth of every person's quest for identity and purpose. Naturally beautiful, gifted and talented she found herself seeking significance in that which was an illusion. The seduction of the enemy's lies almost stole the authentic beauty that laid within. Julie's story will impact and breathe truth into the deceptive side of glamour. For every gorgeous girl searching for that which makes her stand out in a crowd, this book will show you the red carpet to being a true Queen."

Laura Lynn Tyler Thompson
Co-Host of "700 Club Canada"
Host of "Laura Lynn & Friends"

"Julie's story reminds us that behind a bright smile there can be deep pain. Having come through difficulty by her faith in Jesus Christ, Julie shares her testimony in a way that will encourage you to leave your past behind and let God restart you life."

Matt & Lisa Tapley
Lead & Associate Pastors
Lakemount Worship Centre
Grimsby, ON, Canada

"When dealing with discouragement and struggling through life's difficulties and circumstances, it is easy to believe that things will never change. But scripture demonstrates that God loves a big finish, no matter how the story begins. The Author of all-time always writes a happy ending. Julie Stautland is one of those stories – a true testimony to the power and mercy of God to restore a life and create beauty out of ashes."

Brian Warren, Pastor, Teacher, Evangelist
Co-Host of "700 Club Canada"
Pastor of The Hope Centre
Mississauga, ON, Canada

"Julie has led an extraordinary life…the highest highs and devastating lows that could have taken her out. "TRAUMA QUEEN

– A Broken Beauty discovers God's Love" outlines her life and how these experiences led her to a place of total redemption. For the millions who have similar struggles this book will encourage you and give you hope for the amazing future that God has promised."

Rick Cua
Pastoral Care Pastor, Grace Chapel, Leiper's Fork, TN
President/CEO, Kingdom Bound Ministries, Buffalo, NY

Diana Cua
Biblical Counselor
Grace Chapel, Leiper's Fork, TN

INTRODUCTION

L ight. The **power** of light. Even in our own solar system,
every planet is dominated by the magnificent force of the
sun. Radiant beams of light from the sun give life to our whole
planet – to every living cell – plant or creature. Without it we
would all die. Light produces energy that we use for all our
technology in some way or another. We are literally nothing
without light. How fitting it is then that Jesus said, "I am the
light of the world. Whoever follows me will never walk in darkness, but will have the **light** of life." John8:12 (emphasis mine)

As a seven or eight year old, I used to lie in bed at night
and ponder why I was here in this world, what was my purpose in life, and what value did I have as a girl from a modest
family. Like every human being, I was seeking for significance,
self-esteem and security.

My bed had a bookcase headboard with a pull-string light
in the middle of it. Pulling on the string, I would turn on the light
and use it to power up my Sunday school bookmark designed
with a velvet, white cross on it. After about a minute of the
bookmark absorbing the light, I would pull on the string to
return to the natural darkness in my room, only now the velvet,

white cross on my bookmark would brightly glow. It was comforting to lie there in the glow of the cross, as I tried to ignore the water stain on the ceiling that always appeared as an evil face at night. Unfortunately, the glow never lasted very long, so some nights I would repeatedly turn on my light to 'power up' the bookmark until I felt safe and sleepy enough.

Many of those nights as I would stare at the cross, I would question whether or not Jesus was God. In fact, despite my perfect Sunday school attendance, I sometimes questioned if there was a God and did he **really** love little me? Did he do all those miracles? Was the Bible actually true?

It would be years before I found answers. I know I am not alone when it comes to asking these questions. You may be the type of person who comes across as strong, confident and in control, without a care in this world, but in the quiet darkness of the night, you, too, may have your worries and insecurities scream to be heard.

I hope after reading this book that you are encouraged. I desperately desire for you to understand just how much God loves you and how He has a plan specifically for you. If you feel weak and broken, then join me on my journey from damaged goods to God's grace. He won't let you down.

For the sake of writing ease, as well as my protection, many of the names in this book have been changed.

Chapter One

THE EARLY YEARS

"Breathe. Remember to breathe. Calm down stomach. Stand up straight. Shoulders back. *Don't* trip. Smile. Speak clearly and strongly. This is your big moment. This is what you've been working towards. This is your chance to change the course of your life. Now breathe."

It had been a whirlwind week in Toronto with the Miss Teen Canada Pageant contestants. Early mornings had never been my thing and this was testing my ability to be coherent never mind beautiful and pleasant. Dining with the others girls and chaperones was also a challenge because someone would eventually notice how little I was actually eating. The day of the physical fitness test was extra difficult for me as we were all forced to eat the exact same lunch–and *all* of it – before performing our physical fitness tests. I desperately tried to hide the cottage cheese underneath a large piece of romaine lettuce. My stomach ached liked crazy from the shocker of so much food and there was no chance of secretly throwing it all up. How in the world was I going to do well on any test? I never took any gym class in high school. There was **no** way I was going to be sweaty all day. There was nothing pretty about me being sweaty. I had a hard enough time trying to keep the constant oily shine on my face under control. It was not easy trying to hide the repeated patting of paper napkins on my shiny, mirror-like face all day long, and then re-powdering again and again.

It took a *lot* of work to appear like I had it all together. Girls like Jill Hennesey (Miss Teen Kitchener-Waterloo), who starred as the lead in *Jordan's Crossing* from 2001–2007, were so naturally beautifully without a stitch of makeup, and I felt like I had to be a master artist every morning just to try to have a shot.

Even my experience in theatre was not enough to help me deal with a poorly working monitor while performing my solo for the talent portion of the contest. I knew I was struggling to be in tune, but I sang with gusto anyway. Go big or go home. This small town girl with no modeling training was going to show them what an underdog could do!

The most important thing was to appear *confident* and in *control*. No one was to ever know that my heart was still crushed from the harsh break-up of my supposed knight-in-shining-armor just weeks earlier; or that I had never recovered from my date-rape relationship before that; or that I would do absolutely anything to be thin and thinner; or that thoughts of suicide had started to pop into my head because I didn't think it was possible for God to ever forgive me. I wore my 'I got it all together' mask all the time. I had become a character in my own life's performance.

Now I waited backstage for my cue.....'Miss Teen London, Julie vander Maden!'.....It was show time…Time to pretend that I didn't feel like worthless, damaged goods.

One thing I have learned in life is that no matter how good things may appear on the surface in someone else's life, there has usually been some kind of pain that they have had to work through. It could be a broken family, sickness, difficult finances, addictions, or sexual abuse to name a few.

My family isn't any different. My father lost his mother in childbirth to his baby sister when he was only three. His new-born sister was given to an aunt and uncle to be raised. His father remarried and more siblings were born. At ten, his family had to be rescued from Holland's great 1953 flood. They lost everything, so they decided to accept the Christian Reform church's offer to immigrate with several other Dutchmen to Canada. They lived for a year in the backwoods of Cape Breton in a rat-infested house with no running water while my grandfather and eldest uncle, John, worked for a mill cutting wood.

Moving to Strathroy, Ontario was a little better—sometimes. My grandfather was not a happy man. One time he almost beat my dad to death, but thankfully my uncle John intervened. My grandfather was not well educated, so his earnings were never enough to feed the whole family of ten. Uncle John was forced to work for the family, and as soon as the law would allow, my father joined him. A truant officer pulled my father from a job, so that he was forced to finish at least grade nine.

Despite all these trials, what really broke my father was the death of his beloved, older sister, Mary. She was like a mother to him. She died of cancer at the early age of twenty-five. She had only been married nine months. One day my dad visited Mary in the hospital. She requested that he open the window for some fresh air. Shortly afterwards she died of pneumonia and her newlywed husband blamed my father for her death. My dad had a nervous breakdown and was hospitalized. When he recovered, he vowed to marry only someone with the name 'Mary' like his sister. He dated three 'Marys' before marrying my mother. By the way, her name is Mary.

My mother was born the last of six children: three older brothers, a sister and her fraternal, twin sister. We don't know much about my mother's family background because her mother gave all the kids up for adoption in London, Ontario. We believe finances forced her. Unfortunately, my mom had a condition called rickets which meant she had not received enough calcium, vitamin D, or phosphorous in her early development. This condition caused her to be separated from her twin sister and older sister. The couple that adopted her sisters was looking for strong girls to help out on their farm. Mom was too weak for that. In a twist of fate, the wife of the adoptive couple had a sister and husband that also wished to adopt. As this couple lived in Strathroy, a small town, there would be no hard labor for my mother. We have no idea who adopted the older brothers, but although my mother was separated from her twin sister and older sister, by adoption they grew up knowing each other as 'cousins'. Even on my mother's wedding day, she was forced to lie and say her blood sisters were her cousins. Not an easy feat to pull off when she looked so similar to her fraternal twin. Being adopted in my mother's generation was generally not well accepted.

Despite the strangeness of attitude towards adoption, my adoptive grandparents were kind and loving to my mother. The only wrinkle was my adoptive grandmother's sister who also lived full-time with them. She suffered from schizophrenia. At times she was cruel to my mother. On the morning of my mother's wedding, in the heat of an argument, my mother's adoptive aunt burst out with a previously unknown family fact that one of my mother's brothers had committed suicide at the age of twenty.

It was these life experiences that led my father and mother to be drawn to each other in a desperate attempt to escape their present situations. Both were so full of wounds that they tried to find comfort and healing in each other. My father could only find factory work because of his lack of education. This meant that many times throughout my life my father was laid off from work. My mother was able to get into a special hospital training program, despite not having a high school diploma, in order to become a Registered Nurse Assistant. Together they struggled to make a modest life. And that's where I come in. I am the firstborn in my family and my brother was born two years later. I was born with a full head of dark, brown hair. The nurses even made two big finger curls on the front of my head. My mother said that I looked like a china doll. When I look at my baby pictures, I am not sure if that is because my head was round like a bowling ball, or because it was so big that I could not hold it up on my own for a long time.

My brother and I were the typical siblings with the typical fights. The last physical squabble I had with my brother was when I was fourteen and he was twelve. I vividly remember running to the bathroom for my life to lock the door before I received the impact of my brother's rage. Like any brother, he called me many names. The only name that stung deeply and impacted my self-esteem was being called 'Fatso'. I was a slightly chubby kid, but in no stretch of the imagination fat. Yet, I never saw myself as anything but fat from early childhood onwards. Words hurt. Don't let anyone tell you otherwise. My brother never intended to have such a negative impact on my life by saying one little word, but that's all it took. It is amazing the power of our words.

James3:3-10 says, "When we put bits into the mouths of horses to make them obey us, we can turn the whole animal. Or take ships as an example. Although they are so large and are driven by strong winds, they are steered by a very small rudder wherever the pilot wants to go. Likewise, the tongue is a small part of the body, but it makes great boasts. Consider what a great forest is set on fire by a small spark. The tongue also is a fire, and is itself set on fire by hell. All kind of animals, birds, reptiles and sea creatures are being tamed by mankind, but no human being can tame the tongue. It is a restless evil, full of deadly poison. **With the tongue we praise our Lord and Father, and with it we curse human beings, who have been made in God's likeness. Out of the same mouth come praise and cursing. My brothers and sister, this should not be.**"(emphasis mine)

22

Until I was nine, we rented a house that was well over a hundred years old and it looked like it. Our landlord was Dutch like my father and half the town. The other half of the town was Portuguese when I was growing up. I remember genuinely asking my father when I was little, "Why are you not rich like all the other Dutch people in town, Daddy?" Because wherever I looked it seemed like all the Dutch had nice houses, nice cars and nice clothes. We even bought our used cars from Dutchmen. I was so embarrassed to be driven around in one of my father's big tanks. He drove a 1964 blue Dodge until he upgraded to a 1965 red Dodge. I remember sliding back and forth in the huge bench seat with no seatbelts. My brother and I had many fights back there. My poor father. He worked hard. Yet, our house was home not only to my family, but also to field mice, spiders, daddy long legs, silver fish insects and my personal favorite – bats.

On the whole, I was a fairly obedient child. I *hated* having anyone be disappointed with me. I was always scared to break the rules. In school, I was often called a 'goodie two shoes'. One time when I was around three, my father scolded me for not using my fork in the proper hand while eating my spaghetti at lunchtime. He told me that if I couldn't eat using my fork in the proper hand then I might as well climb a tree. So, obediently after lunch I went outside and climbed a tree. Minutes later, I came in crying with my belly all scraped and bleeding. My mother asked me what happened. I told her that Daddy said I should climb a tree if I couldn't use my fork properly. Clearly it would be awhile before I stopped taking things literally.

Of course, I am a firstborn with a strong stubborn streak, too. In this particular incident, I don't know what came over me because my actions were so out of character. I was four years old and graduating from junior Sunday school. All I had to do was smile in the group picture wearing my white graduation gown and hat. The reward was a huge chunk of chocolate for every child. For some reason there was *no* way I was going to have my picture taken with the class. I fully understood the consequences of not receiving my precious chocolate, but I could not be persuaded. My parents have a lovely picture of me standing on my ankles, in my white graduation gown and hat, frowning.

As you see, I was no different than any other child. There was a part of me that wanted to please, so that I would find love and acceptance, and then there was a part of me that wanted to do my own thing, my own way. Like I've heard so many times before, no parent struggles with their toddler agreeably answering 'yes' too often, or having to stop their toddler from being too kind and sharing too much. Instead, the words 'no' and 'mine' are much more frequently verbalized by that adorable little person. It's pretty obvious that there is no perfect, angelic child, but rather every one of us is born with an inherited self-centered, sinful nature.

1John 1:8 says, "If we claim to be without sin, we deceive ourselves and the truth is not in us."

Even though I believe we are born with a sin nature, I believe we are also born with God-given traits and characteristics. And there begins the battle for our souls. It's so easy for us to make everything about 'me me me or I I I'. I believe we have to fight to develop our God-given traits. These traits can only take deep root when we choose to relinquish control of our own will over to Christ.

Later in grade one, I had an interesting battle with my own perception of what was 'right and wrong'. I put up with an annoying little boy who dressed poorly, smelled, picked on people and always got into trouble. One day he even cut a piece of my hair off as he walked by my desk. I am telling you all this so you understand that I had no 'love' for Chuck.

In our grade one classroom we were fortunate to have our own class bathroom. Miss Stacy, our teacher, was nice, but one day she had had enough. On more than one occasion someone had taken their big primary pencil and drawn on the inside of the toilet bowl. Weird, I know, but remember it was grade one. Kids do strange things. Chuck had been disciplined before for doing this, but I guess this time Miss Stacy did not want to assume he was to blame again. Instead she said that the whole class would not be allowed to have lunch and go outside to play until the person confessed. She told us to all put our heads down on our desks and asked the person responsible to raise their hand. Then the remaining class would be allowed to eat lunch and go outside to play. Well, everyone *knew* it was Chuck again, but eternity seemed to pass and he *still* hadn't raised his hand. My six–year–old righteous and indignant anger was slowly rising up within me while I thought about how unfair it was for the *whole* class to be punished for his crime. Finally I couldn't take it any longer and I decided to sacrifice myself for the class. I put up my hand to accept the blame for the toilet bowl scribbling. Miss Stacy was shocked. The class was shocked. And more importantly, I was shocked. What was I thinking? I was the 'goodie two shoes'. I was terrified of getting into trouble and here I was taking the blame for something *I did not do.*

Baffled and bewildered, Miss Stacy took me aside while the rest of the class got to eat their lunch and go outside. She asked me why I would do such a thing and I made up a super lame story. I said that I forgot my pencil was in my hand when I had to use the bathroom earlier, and the pencil accidentally fell into the toilet, marking the sides as it went in. She asked me to repeat my story several times because it was obvious that she didn't believe me. I am still amazed that this shy little version of myself would do such a bold thing. But I thought I was standing up for justice. I hated things not being fair.

I don't think we appreciate the fact it wasn't 'fair' that Jesus had to die for *our* sins (selfishness, stubbornness, and the list of negative traits goes on) when he did nothing wrong. Christians recite that Jesus was born of a virgin and died on the cross for our sins and rose on the third day. It's so easy to just rattle off those words, but how often do we really stop to let the weight of those words impact us. Jesus *chose* to go to the cross for something he didn't do. Think about that. I cannot get my head around that thought when I know how much a silly paper cut hurts. Never mind enduring flesh ripping lashings, beatings, thorns pressed into your head, walking with a huge wooden cross all the way up to Golgatha hill, and *then* being nailed and hung on a cross to die – all for something you *didn't* do! Hello? Anyone with me on this? Do you know anyone who would be willing to do that for you? We know the answer already. Think about how deep God's love is for us, and yet we are just little ants clinging to a dirt ball in space. The bible says that Jesus died to set us free. That means freedom has a price tag on it. And the price tag for the freedom of our souls was the sacrificial death of a perfect, sinless God clothed in humanity – Jesus Christ.

Romans8:35-39 says, "Who shall separate us from the love of Christ? Shall trouble or hardship or persecution or famine or nakedness or danger or sword? As it is written:

'For your sake we face death all day long;
we are considered as sheep to be slaughtered.'

No, in all these things we are more than conquerors through him who loved us. For I am convinced that neither death nor life, neither angels nor demons, neither the present nor the future, nor any powers, neither height nor depth, nor anything else in all creation, will be able to separate us from the love of God that is in Christ Jesus our Lord."

My grade two teacher, Miss Clare, was tall with straight, long blonde hair. She was beautiful, but she was like Snow White's evil stepmother. Her personality made all her outer beauty fade. All the kids were scared of her. She used to walk up and down the desk aisles and drill the tip of her pen into a student's head if she disapproved of something. One time I had to stay inside at lunchtime because of a cold or something. Miss Clare told me and another boy that she had to briefly leave the room. Under no circumstances were we allowed to leave the room. Well, she didn't return until the end of lunchtime. I sat at my desk desperately needing to go to the bathroom, but I didn't dare leave the room. I finally couldn't hold it a second longer and I literally peed my pants. I could never look at that boy the same again. I was so ashamed and embarrassed. And of course, I suffered the wrath of Miss Clare when she finally returned to the classroom.

On another occasion in grade two, I followed the lead of other kids sliding down a small ice hill during lunchtime. On my turn, I slid and slammed my face flat on the ice. My nose was bleeding, my lips were cut and bleeding and everything was swollen. Miss Clare refused my request to call my mother and instead forced me to sit through class the rest of the day. When my mother saw my distorted, swollen face after school, boy, did the principal get an ear-full from her.

I was scared to read out loud in class, too, because I would stumble over my words. I used to mix up my words when I would have to speak. I had to work on not fumbling my words for years. My self-confidence in grade two was really low. Miss Clare did nothing to help my self-esteem either. It seemed like she hated kids. I am not sure why Miss Clare was so mean to her students, but I am sure there must have been something in her life that made her behave so.

My grade three teacher was much nicer. I started to have a little faith in my developing intellect, too. I was very proud to hold the title as one of the quickest to answer addition, subtraction, multiplication and division facts in my class' 'Around the World' math game. I could take on anybody! Grade three also presented me with a gift that I wish I could refuse – the start of my battle with acne. Fortunately, it was not a severe type of cystic acne, just mild breakouts across my forehead that would over the years travel down my face, chest, back and arms. A battle that I am still trying to win to this day, even while I fight newly appearing wrinkles. Boy, was my dermatologist wrong! She said that with my oily skin I would not get many wrinkles. Wrong. No, instead, I have oily skin, a little acne AND wrinkles. And, yes, you can still catch me patting down my face with paper napkins and re-applying another layer of fresh face powder. Yup. It's so much fun.

Even though I wished for a nicer house growing up, I enjoyed the two huge weeping willow trees out front. We used those trees to make tree forts, and swings. I felt like I was entering my own private world when I walked underneath the hanging branches, or while I sat up in the trunk of the tree and watched the neighborhood around me. It was so much fun swinging on the weeping willow branches. That is, until the branches eventually broke, and I landed with a thud on the ground. The worst thing was falling out of the tree. That happened a couple times at least. I remember lying on the ground, flat on my back, with the wind knocked out of me, staring up into the swaying branches of the willow tree. If you've ever had something similar happen to you, then you know the frantic feeling you experience as you wait anxiously for your lungs to inflate.

Sometimes God allows us to symbolically fall flat on our backs in order to get our attention. There are times when we, even as Christians, can be so absorbed in our own business that we don't realize He has been trying to get our attention, or trying to redirect us for His greater purpose. What we are absorbed in might be wonderful work, but if we plow ahead and don't remember to let God lead our lives, *watch out.* Sometimes He will give us a tough love reminder. What we do with His reminder is more important. Do you get angry and try to force your own way in the situation anyway? I have definitely been guilty of that. Or do you receive the wake-up call and re-evaluate what you should be doing?

James 4:15-17 says, "Instead, you ought to say, "If it is the Lord's will, we will live and do this or that. As it is, you boast in your arrogant schemes. All such boasting is evil. If anyone, then, knows the good they ought to do and doesn't do it, it is sin for them."

I started this chapter with a recap of the dialog running through my head as I was backstage waiting to hear my name be called for the beginning of the Miss Teen Canada 1985 pageant. As you will discover, several incidences led up to this high/low point in my life. One of my methods of coping with life as a teenager was to write poetry. Fortunately, I was able to find my book of old poems, so throughout my book you will be able to read some of the emotionally raw writings during my youth.

I'll end this chapter with a poem that was written a few months after I recommitted my life to Christ at 18 years old. It shares how despite the scars I attained growing up, the light of Jesus was shining in me. I was beginning the healing process with Jesus in my heart and guiding my life.

THE LITTLE GIRL

Written January 1986

On Grandma's lap she sat,
While Grandma's fingers ran through the little girl's hair.
With the eyes the size of quarters,
The little girl shone from within.
Ignorant to her purpose in life,
The little girl enjoyed the moment,
Unaware of the future's destiny.

Spinning, spinning forward in time,
The little girl has grown up.
Grandma no longer offers her lap,
Or plays with the girl's hair.
The girl is no longer ignorant or unaware.
Scars are visible on her soul,
But, alas, her eyes the size of quarters,
Still shine from within.

Julie vander Maden

MOMENTS OF REFLECTION

At the end of each chapter, I would like you to take some time to reflect on your own life. Write down your thoughts, memories, feelings and scriptures. This process can help to put things into perspective. You may realize that you need to forgive someone, or that you need to ask for forgiveness. The

Holy Spirit may bring a scripture to your mind, or give you a new insight into an old problem. Whatever it is, I pray that taking a few moments to reflect will help to deepen your relationship with Jesus.

What kind of family situation did your own parents grow up in?

How has your parents' upbringing affected how they have raised you?

Do you feel that you have taken advantage of the wisdom they have gleaned from their life own experiences?

Have you forgiven them for making any bad choices in the past that you feel has negatively affected your childhood?

Have you set your moral compass upon God's word, the Bible, or do you find yourself 'winging it' through any moral dilemmas you face?

Have people's words ever hurt you? How have you responded?

Have you ever hurt people with your own cutting words? Have you tried to repair the damage you caused with those words?

Do you find it so easy to be stubborn and 'dig your heels in' even when you know that you are wrong? Or are you always teachable?

Have you ever stopped to think just how much Jesus loves **you**?

Willingly giving us the gift of eternal life cost Jesus the price of pain, suffering, and finally, death. Have you, or someone close to you, willingly suffered or sacrificed to help someone else?

Chapter Two

SO THIS IS JESUS?

As our Sunday school class began to wrap up for church service, Linda called us to attention. "Ok, now, before everyone leaves, Tom and I would like to invite you to a party. We would like everyone to meet at Tom's house on Saturday, two weeks from now, for a Jesus Party."

The class rumbled with questions, "A Jesus party? What's that? I've never heard of that before! Did you say—on a Saturday? What do you do at a Jesus party? Will it be fun?"

"Ok, ok, I understand you have a lot of questions. Yes, it will be fun. Please take this information sheet with you to get your parents' permission, and please return it next Sunday. I really hope you all can make it."

Grade four was the year of new beginnings. We bought a house (from a Dutchmen, of course) about a mile outside of Strathroy, and became best friends with our new (Dutch) neighbors. I got an amazing new teacher at school. And even at my church two teenagers, who I had never seen before, became my new Sunday school teachers. Life was definitely improving.

My parents still live in the house they bought when I was nine. It wasn't new when we bought it, but there were way less bugs, and most importantly, no bats compared to our other house. It wasn't very big, but at least I got my own room. And I was happy to see a tall, weeping willow tree on our new front lawn. Even though my father would be laid off from work sometimes, my mother managed to save up enough for a down payment on the house. She had set up a separate bank account in London a half hour drive away. Yes, this was before the popularity of ATMs. That way she wouldn't be tempted to touch the money. She would always make deposits on Saturdays, so I loved coming along for the ride. I knew there might be some shopping, or at least an ice cream, or McDonald's to look forward to. Some of my favorite memories with my mom are when we would go through a McDonald's drive-thru after making her Saturday deposit. During McDonald's Monopoly game season, we would buy one food item at the drive-thru, so we could get a game sticker. Since you were only allowed one game sticker per purchase per hour, we would then find another McDonald's to purchase a different food item. Over two or three hours we eventually ate a burger, fries, drink and a sundae. The best part was letting my mom order at the speaker. For some reason she would get the giggles and just lose it. Sometimes I would have to finish placing the order because my mom was giggling so much that she couldn't speak.

At school a new teacher was newly employed and she just happened to be the principal's daughter. She was tall, pretty and smiled a lot. I was thrilled to have her as my teacher. Miss Wallace quickly saw something in me that I couldn't see myself–potential.

That year my grades soared to the top of the class. All thanks to the wonderful encouragement of Miss Wallace. She trusted me to even be class monitor. I was so honored. And although my acne began to spread from my forehead downwards, I managed to overcome my nervousness to recite my first class speech without forgetting or fumbling over any words. Not only that, I was elected to speak in the school competition. I placed 2nd in the whole school. I went on to enter the local Legion public speaking contest and won first place. All for speaking about the time when my cat Daisy got her leg accidentally cut off by a car fan belt. That year I also won the school science fair contest with my partner and the proceeding year as well. It was amazing. Who was this person? It couldn't be me.

My mother encouraged me to start taking piano lessons. I really wasn't that interested in piano, but I had a wonderful teacher, Dalton Walpole. He was already retired when I started, but he lived until just a few years ago. I was never much good at playing, and I always refused to cut my long nails. Dalt always said that the clicking of my nails was my second percussion instrument. He threatened every week to have nail clippers ready to cut my nails, but he never did. He was so sweet and kind. When we played duets together, sometimes our hands would touch and my hands were always cold. He would stop playing, take my cold hands in his and say, 'You know what they say about cold hands? You must have a warm heart." His favorite music to play was ragtime and he loved to compose his own ragtime music. Even though I was far from being one of his better students, the greatest gift he gave me was my own ragtime titled '*Meet Miss Julie*'.

What I really enjoyed was to sing, so my mother let me start classical vocal lessons that year, too. Ms Harper had a beautiful, full voice and I was intimidated with my quiet, breathy voice. Thankfully, she was very patient with me. I quickly realized that I loved to perform for the sake of people's enjoyment, but I *hated* performing every year for Kiwanis music festivals. At these competitions I cringed while the judges publically picked apart my technical performance. It crushed my confidence, whereas receiving the applause after a musical performance was exhilarating. I wanted more of it.

I mentioned that at church two new teenagers became Sunday school teachers my grade four year. I must admit we didn't have an abundance of young people at our church. I can still see the organist hunched over the organ. She taught *my* mother to play the piano when she was a little girl. The organist looked like her whole body had become one with the organ. I think they must have had to peel her off the organ bench when she finally retired. Our minister was a very polite, white-haired, soft-spoken man who easily put me to sleep during his sermons. The church I grew up in was far from lively or interesting. And until that year, most teachers were sweet, older ladies who used very dry teaching material. Having new blood show up to teach Sunday school was exciting.

Tom and Linda were a breath of fresh air. I couldn't believe how excited they were about Jesus. I mean, these two teenagers actually acted like Jesus was alive and doing miraculous stuff through prayer today. How was that possible? And they weren't making it up. They really truly believed that they had a *personal* relationship with Jesus where they could talk to Him as a friend. And you know what was crazier? They believed Jesus answered them back through the Holy Spirit.

They shared with us that we, too, could know Jesus personally as our friend and savior if we would just pray and ask him to forgive us of our sins and to enter our heart. My church taught me that I was a Christian because I was sprinkled with water during a baby baptism. And we went to church service every Sunday, so I thought that was enough.

That year I looked forward to going to church every week. I mean, I always had perfect Sunday school attendance before then, but it wasn't because I was having a fantastic time or anything. Tom and Linda even invited us over to Tom's house one Saturday for a Jesus party. I thought it was the weirdest thing. Who talks about Jesus every day of the week? God already had my Sunday morning, but I went and had a great time. Wow. I didn't know this was what being a Christian could be like. And they told us stories about people who were healed miraculously through prayer. I so wanted to believe it all.

Before that year finished, I had accepted Jesus as my Lord and Savior. I was excited and hungry to learn more about Jesus and what it was like to live as a Christian. Tom and Linda greatly impacted my life. I am so grateful that they were willing to take a chance teaching my class. You see, Tom and Linda were no longer teaching Sunday school when I returned in September, my grade five year. It wasn't until I was fourteen that I found out the whole story why they didn't continue teaching. Tom and Linda were actually members of another church in town. They both felt led of the Holy Spirit to attend my church for morning service and to teach Sunday school. They knew my church was not giving clear, solid teaching about how to become a real, vibrant Christian. They hoped to reach some of the youth in my church. On Sunday evening, they would attend their own church. Well, when my church found out where they really belonged, and what they were teaching us – out the door they went. 'What! Teaching kids to ask Jesus into their hearts? Crazy.'

I wish I could say that I stood strong and continued to grow in the Lord, but I found myself becoming so frustrated. There were so many unanswered questions from my Sunday school teachers after Tom and Linda were asked to leave. They just didn't have the answers. Over time my zeal for Jesus wore off, and slowly, as I started to make bad choices, God became like a big cop in the sky to me—but more on that later.

At the end of my grade four school year, Miss Wallace told our class that she would not be returning the following September to teach at our school. The class gasped. Everyone loved her. I knew she might not be my teacher in the fall, but at least I counted on her being around to talk to whenever I needed. How could she leave us? After waiting for all of us to calm down, she smiled and said, "I'm getting married over the summer, so Mrs. Millcroft will be a new teacher in the fall." We asked if she knew Mrs. Millcroft. She said, "Yes, quite well. Mrs. Millcroft will be my married name." We all cheered.

You can imagine my excitement when I found out newly named Mrs. Millcroft was going to teach a split grade four/five class. Thankfully, grade five was to be a continuation of receiving her wonderful encouragement.

MOMENTS OF REFLECTION

Can you name someone who has greatly impacted and inspired you? A parent, teacher, Sunday teacher, coach, friend, celebrity?

What made that person stand out so much from the rest of the crowd?

Have you implemented any of the wisdom or life lessons you learned from that person?

Do you know if you have been a source of inspiration to anyone around you?

What have you tried to model for that person?

If you are a Christian, do you believe you have the same passion and courage to break out of normal routines like Tom and Linda did, in order to let God use you?

If you don't know Jesus yet as your personal Lord and Savior, I would like to invite you to read John 3:16 in the Bible first, and then read all of the book of John. The book of John is a great place to hear about God's love for each of us.

Chapter Three

SEEKING MY FATHER'S LOVE

"Ice cream

Is anything more delectable

Than ice cream?

Why, even the most respectable

Eat ice cream

It's wonderful on a summer's afternoon

In June......."

I belted out my song as Diana Barry with as much enthusiasm as possible. I was soaking up my moment in the spotlight. The audience enthusiastically clapped. Wow, how I loved this.

I tried out for the school play and managed to be the youngest student to get a lead role. I auditioned for the role of Diana Barry in *Anne of Green Gables*. I can still see the shock on the teachers' faces as they watched my audition of Diana mistakenly get drunk on cordial. Because I was only ten and in grade five while the girl who played Anne was a tall, thirteen year old in grade eight, I had to wear heels so that I didn't look so short standing beside her. That was the beginning of my acting career. No one knew I had it in me, but going on stage was like entering a magical world for me. Singing and acting became my passion.

I continued to work hard at my schoolwork in every subject during my grade six year. I was definitely competitive and I always expected the most out of myself. I had my few close friends and we enjoyed many fun sleepovers. There is only one incident that stands out in my memory about grade six.

In the winter, during our lunch recess, one of the boys in my class decided it would be really funny to knock me down in the snow. I can't remember how he tricked me into going around the corner of the school building where kids normally didn't go during recess. But before I knew what was happening, he jumped on top of me, pinning me to the ground with the full weight of his body. He then proceeded to thrust himself on top of me. I screamed and struggled, but no one came over to us. When he was finally done, he got up and started to walk away. Laughing, he turned and said, "You know you liked it." We may have both been bundled up in our heavy winter clothes, but I can't tell you how violated I felt. Shaking all over, I found a couple of my friends and we headed for the school bathroom. Then I went to pieces. I began crying uncontrollably. I was angry, I was scared, I was embarrassed and I was violated. How dare he do such a thing and think it was a big joke? Besides my close friends, I didn't want to talk to anyone about the incident. I gained my composure and returned to class. Sexual abuse can happen in many forms. In retrospect, I should have squealed on him to the teacher or principal, but I was so embarrassed I couldn't bring myself to it.

In grade seven I was once again chosen to compete in the school public speaking contest. The morning of the competition, I woke up with the stomach flu. I remember being all dressed up and sitting on the floor with my head resting on the toilet seat. In between vomiting, I debated whether or not to pick myself up off the floor and head out for the bus stop anyway. I wasn't going to win the contest sitting by the toilet; that was for sure. I knew the contest began at one in the afternoon, so if I could just manage to make it through the morning, then I could compete. I made up my mind and went to school. I threw up a couple times in the morning and I prayed like crazy that I wouldn't throw up during the competition. I really needed that prayer to be answered because the teachers decided to have all the contestants sit on stage while each one took their turn speaking. I prayed to be chosen to speak first and my prayer was answered. I spoke, mustering all the strength I could to sound animated, loud and clear. I managed not to blank out. I finished and sat down in the chair. I made it, but not for long. When the next person started to speak, I had to race off stage to the bathroom again. Once everyone finished speaking, I was shocked to hear my name declared as the winner. When I confessed to the hosting teacher that I had the stomach flu and that she should not get too close to me, she couldn't believe I had done such an amazing job. Before I could say another word, she put her arm around me and announced to everyone in the auditorium that I had competed with the stomach flu. (So much for keeping that a secret.) I was so glad that I forced myself, but afterwards, I just wanted to crash at home with my mom's flat ginger ale and jello home remedies.

I continued to excel in my middle school grades. I won more science project awards. I competed every year in the school public speaking contests and placed at the District finals. I performed the character Becky Thatcher in our school play *'Tom Sawyer'*. I sang at my graduation. I was driven to do better and better at everything I did. I even got a part-time job at the flower greenhouse, straight across from our house that managed only to pay me peanuts. I wish I could say that it was all for the right reasons, but it wasn't. You see, despite the fact that Mrs. Millcroft, Dalt, Ms Harper, my friends and others wholeheartedly believed in me, I was seeking the approval of only one person, my father. My mother had always been my biggest fan, but I yearned for my father's attention and approval.

When my brother and I were born, my father made it clear to my mother that she was to do all the disciplining in our childhood. He made that decision because he knew he had inherited his father's struggle with anger. My father was usually too laid back instead of pushy, so he tended to be passive/aggressive. If he was pushed too far, that's when he found it difficult to control his response to anger. Instead of learning ways to cope with his feelings, he decided to just avoid any potentially negative situation. It was his way of protecting my brother and me from himself. As a consequence to his decision, he naturally took a back seat in our family. His own father was never affectionate and his mother died at three, so he didn't know how to openly express his love towards us. As a child, that translated into 'not caring" or 'not finding me worthwhile enough'. I could always joke with my father, but I could never go to him for advice or guidance. He never said the words "I love you." My mother attended everything I did, but because of work, or just being too tired, my father missed many events in my life. Time and time again, I would leave my trophy or ribbon on the kitchen table for him to see when he got home from work. Hoping upon hope that he would leave me a note saying something like, "Great job. I'm so proud of you. I love you." But he never did. I know now that he was always proud of me, but back then he just didn't know how to express his feelings so I could understand his love. I always walked away feeling like it wasn't enough for him. I felt like I wasn't good enough for him. This drove me to try harder–to work harder.

Just like I desperately yearned for my father's love and approval, every single one of us yearns for our Heavenly Father's love whether we realize it or not. If we don't fill this hole inside of us with God's love as He designed, we will fill it with whatever we can find. Maybe we become obsessed about our body image; or addicted to having the newest and latest thing on the market; or driven to become as rich as possible; or obsessed with becoming famous and powerful. It could be any number of things we try to fill in the hole that God created in human beings. The void that can only be satisfied with God Himself residing.

I think it is important at this point to take some time and talk about how God views us. I what to show you a few scriptures that reveal more about how much God loves us, and how He views us as His precious children. These scriptures greatly impacted me on my journey to healing and restoration.

God doesn't create worthless junk. You might be thinking, "Well, you don't know me. That sounds good for someone else, but I don't see how that can pertain to me." I don't have to know you personally because God has *always* known and loved you!

Psalm139:13-16 "For you created my inmost being; you knit me together in my mother's womb. **I praise you because I am fearfully and wonderfully made**; your works are wonderful, I know that full well. My frame was not hidden from you when I was made in the secret place, when I was woven together in the depths of the earth. Your eyes saw my unformed body; all the days ordained for me were written in your book before one of them came to be."(emphasis mine)

So there you go. No matter what the circumstances were behind how or why you came into this world, *you* were not an accident! You were known and loved before you were ever born. That doesn't sound like worthless junk to me.

If we were worthless junk, then why would He create us in *His* image?

Genesis1:27 "**So God created mankind in his own image, in the image of God he created them; male and female he created them.**"(emphasis mine) ·

Hello? Did you get that? God created us in the image of Himself, so obviously there is a *huge* void in our lives if we choose to *ignore* Him and fill it with everything else under the sun.

God cares about every person, no matter how far away from Him they may be.

Matthew18:12-14 (Jesus speaking) "What do you think? If a man owns a hundred sheep, and one of them wanders away, will he not leave the ninety-nine on the hills and go to look for the one that wandered off? And if he finds it, truly I tell you, he is happier about that one sheep than about the ninety-nine that did not wander off. In the same way **your Father in heaven is not willing that any of these little ones should perish.**"(emphasis mine)

God is eagerly waiting to receive you and restore you. You may have heard or read Jesus' parable of the lost son before in the book of Luke. Once the son spent all his inheritance that he forced his father to give to him prematurely, he realized that he made an enormous mistake and *regretted* his actions.

Luke15:17-20 "When **he came to his senses**, he said, 'How many of my father's hired servants have food to spare, and here I am starving to death! I will set out and go back to my father and say to him: Father, I have sinned against heaven and against you. I am no longer worthy to be called your son; make me like one of your hired servants.' So he got up and went to his father. **But while he was still a long way off, his father saw him and was filled with compassion for him; he ran to his son, threw his arms around him and kissed him.**"(emphasis mine)

You see, God doesn't care what horrible, awful, out-of-this-world thing you have done. If you *regret* what you have done and you truly want to *turn away* from it – that is called *repentance*. God will come running towards you with open arms, anxious to grab a hold of you and kiss you with the kiss of compassion and forgiveness. Now that is amazing.

God is our provider. Matthew6:25-33 (Jesus speaking) "Therefore I tell you, do not worry about your life, what you will eat or drink; or about your body, what you will wear. Is not life more than food, and the body more than clothes? Look at the birds of the air; they do not sow or reap or store away in barns, and yet your heavenly Father feeds them. **Are you not much more valuable than they?** Can any one of you by worrying add a single hour to your life? And why do you worry about clothes? See how the flowers of the field grow. They do not labor or spin. Yet I tell you that not even Solomon in all his splendor was dressed like one of these. If that is how God clothes the grass of the field, which is here today and tomorrow is thrown into the fire, will he not much more clothe you- you of little faith? So do not worry, saying, 'What shall we eat?' or 'What shall we drink?' or 'What shall we wear?' For the pagans run after all these things, and your heavenly Father know that you need them. But seek first his kingdom and his righteousness, and all these things will be given to you as well."(emphasis mine)

Whether we have earthly fathers that provide well for us or not, God is ultimately our heavenly Father and He promises to provide for us if we follow him.

God calls us his children. 1John3:1-2 "See what great love the Father has lavished on us, that we should be called **children of God**! And that is what we are! The reason the world does not know us is that it did not know him. Dear friends, now we are **children of God**, and what we will be has not yet been

49

made known. But we know that when Christ appears, we shall be like him, for we shall see him as he is."(emphasis mine)

When we choose to acknowledge that this life is more than just what we see with our physical eyes; when we realize that there is a hole that only God can fill; when we understand that no matter how 'nice and good' we are, we are truly wretched human beings that need a savior; when we surrender our self-control, ask Jesus to forgive us, and accept the work Jesus accomplished by dying on the cross in our place, then, and only then, do we finally find our rightful place in this world. Only then are we able to find true love, joy, and everlasting peace doing whatever it is that God leads us to do. Only then will we know who we are, why we are here, and what we are to do.

This life is our training ground for bigger and better things to come in heaven. This life is preparation. No, if we give our hearts to Jesus, that does *not* mean we will be sitting around on clouds playing harps. Please, let's not insult God. He made the entire universe, so I think we should have some grander ideas of what life in eternity will be like. Our life here is but a vapor.

James4:14 "Why, you do not even know what will happen tomorrow. What is your life? **You are a mist that appears for a little while and then vanishes."**

MOMENTS OF REFLECTION

What is your relationship like with your father or mother?

Do you find yourself seeking approval and self-worth from other people?

Do you trust that God wants the best for you even if your current situation may not be very positive at the moment?

Do you trust that God has a plan for you and a purpose for you life?

Are you living only for the moment, or do you consider what God wants to do in you for the future?

Have you truly turned away (repented) from all the wrong thoughts and actions (sins) that you have done? Or are you keeping some areas to yourself and not letting God in?

How do you view yourself? Do you see yourself through God's eyes, as the scriptures tell us, or are you looking through your own lens?

Do you believe you are precious in the sight of God, or just worthless junk?

Do you sometimes find it difficult to apply God's truth to your life, but find it easy to apply to someone else's?

Chapter Four

EATING DISORDERS TAKE CENTER STAGE

Teenage Years
Written August, 1981, a month before my 14th birthday, about my struggle to grow up faster than my parents wanted me to.

As the years pass by,
And you reach the teen age,
Many new emotions arise to puzzle and boggle your mind,
The need for love and affection is changed,
Leaving home may become a regular routine,
Seeing friends,
Seeing personal friends,
Is your main desire and crave,
Your love for your parents is not changed,
Only approached differently,
Understanding one another is hard and irritating,
But because of your eternal love for your parents,
You will make it through this challenging age.

Julie vander Maden

At the end of grade seven, I had had enough of being 'Fatso' as my brother used to call me. Over that summer before starting grade eight, I decided to do something about it. I began cutting out double portions even if it was my favorite food. It worked. I lost my baby fat and I looked trim and slim like most of the girls when I sang at my grade eight graduation. I liked the feeling of control over my body. I liked feeling more confident, even though I still struggled with my acne.

Eating healthier portions was not a bad thing, but the change in attitude towards my body image was not a good one. Over the summer before entering the new world of high school, fear began to creep into my mind about how well I would be accepted. My best friend at the time was also my next–door neighbor, and together we worked across the road at the flower greenhouse. During the school year we worked Saturday mornings, but in the summer we worked Monday through Friday. While de-budding carnations and weeding summer annuals, we frequently shared our anxieties about entering high school.

Since being the best at everything was my driving goal, the increased pressure of competing against so many students created anxiety that I wouldn't be able to keep up. Maybe I really didn't have the brains to be top of the class in high school. I was terrified of being a nobody. Just a small town girl struggling with acne and weight issues from a modest home. Although it may sound trivial to most people, believe me, it consumed me.

At the same time I met my first love, Tom, a tall, wavy, blonde, Dutch boy. I met him in the spring at the Portuguese dance hall. He was two years older than me, incredibly shy and cute. Meeting Tom gave me another reason to keep the weight off. I never had trouble with boys liking me, even if my brother did call me 'Fatso'. But Tom was different. I fell really hard for him.

THE FIRST TIME WE MET
Written August 4th, 1982 after dating Tom for almost a year.

Dressed to kill, we sit and wait,
Glancing around, we look for bait.
One by one they stare and look,
It's like reading a boring book.
At last I come upon a hot one,
Maybe I'll finally have some fun.
Shyly, he walks up to me,
I think I actually found the key.

My heart begins to pound and pound,
I don't think my feet are touching the ground.
Politely, he asks me to dance,
I answer, "Yes!" in one hot instance.
Behind me, he walks to the dance floor,
My innocent passion rises more.
The music begins to loudly play,
With arms around me, we dance our way.

Sitting at the table are Mom and Dad,
I really hope that they aren't mad.

But as I look at his face,
I thank the Lord for His grace.
With an easy smile, we continue to sway,
I never knew this was my lucky day.
Soon the music is over and done,
Too bad I can't repeat that one.

At the table, we sit and discuss,
All about the ones who asked us.
Finally the disc jockey announces the last dance,
I look over at him with an urgent glance.
He slowly walks up to me again,
Now I wish for my flowing mane.
Once on the floor, we chat some more,
My heart can't help but strongly soar.

I must see him again, but I don't know how,
I can't seem to think of a way right now.
I watch him as he gets in the car,
I wonder if his house is far?
A little depressed, we drive away.
I desperately hope I see him again some day.
Julie vander Maden

The more I thought about failing in high school, the more I decided that I better turn my attention towards my looks. I started dieting seriously over the summer. I also started fighting with my parents frequently. I was desperately trying to grow up fast and they were desperately trying to slow me down. The more I fought with them, the more satisfaction I found in dieting. A new sense of power and control started to sweep over me as I determined what I would eat, when I would eat and how much I would eat. My parents may have been trying to 'ruin my life', but at least they couldn't control my eating habits.

The middle of grade nine I auditioned for the high school musical *'Anything Goes'* by Guy Bolton and P.G. Wodehouse, music by Cole Porter. I got a small part, which was to be expected for a miner niner, but I would be singing and dancing in several scenes, so I was excited. Being involved with the play also meant numerous after school rehearsals until our performance days in May. This gave me plenty of opportunity to be away from my family at mealtime. I was ecstatic. They had been nagging me for a while to eat, eat, eat! I couldn't take it any longer. Nothing was going to stop me from controlling my weight. Absolutely *nothing.*

I decided that I needed to be even thinner, so I only ate every other day. I only allowed a few sips of water from the school fountain as well, because I was completely obsessed with having the flattest stomach possible. I was afraid that even liquid would make me look fat and ruin the look of my stomach. I remember staring at other people's stomachs and comparing them to mine. I even walked around most of the day sucking my stomach in, not that I needed to.

On the days I did eat, I didn't choose to eat healthy. I figured that if any food was going in my mouth, I better like it. With so many rehearsals running over dinnertime, it was easy to walk down to the local ice cream parlor and buy myself a baby chocolate sundae. It was called a baby sundae because it was portioned for babies. It was really small, but it was ice cream and it had chocolate covering it, so I was happy. That was the kind of nutritious food I was eating. On Friday nights I always met my boyfriend, Tom, at the roller-skating rink, so I would never eat until I came home. On those nights I would eat an ice cream bar before going to bed. That would be my meal for the day.

The reality of my anorexia eating disorder sunk into my parents when they saw me on performance night. In one scene I wore a full length, form-fitting gown that showed off how rake thin I had become. They were mortified. Once the production was over, they were determined that my life was going to change.

Since grade eight, I had lost over 30% of my body weight. I went from being a normal 129lbs down to my lowest of 87lbs. And I thought that having my ribs stick out looked great. My menstrual cycle ceased for a year and a half because my weight went too low. My grades went down because I had trouble thinking clearly. I started to develop downy hair on my arms because I was not able to keep my body temperature high enough. But I thought I was finally beautiful. I was so proud of my achievement. This was truly an amazing feat. And no one was going to take it away from me. No one.

The summer before grade ten commenced, my parents had a plan to make sure I ate more. Once again my dad was laid off from work, so he was in charge of making sure that I ate lunch everyday. The only problem was that they did not understand the devious thinking of the anorexic brain. ' Where there is a will, there is a way', as the saying goes. My father tended to spend most of his time outside doing stuff around the yard, so it was easy to get around their new rule. While he was outside, I would pull out a lunch plate, take out a slice of bread, use a knife to scrape some breadcrumbs onto the plate, and then return the slice of bread to the bag. Next I would dip my knife in the butter, then the jam, and place the dirty knife on the lunch plate. Next, I would pull out a glass, pour a little milk in it, swish the milk around, and then pour it out. Lastly, in order to truly make it look believable that I ate, I would take a chocolate cookie and break some cookie crumbs on the lunch plate. Tada. It looked like I ate lunch. I would purposely leave the dirty dishes on the counter as evidence, so when he would come in and say, "Ok, it's time to eat," I would just show him my dishes and say, "I already had lunch."

They never found out about my food tricks, which made me all the happier. Nagging me to eat all the time didn't stop though. It was a constant battle. One I was determined not to lose.

I always enjoyed writing poetry, but now it had become my only outlet to express my inner torment. I would ponder the purpose of life and question the existence of God. I would pour my soul into these poems. Sometimes I would share my poetry with my mother even though she found some of my writings quite disturbing. Little did she, or I know at the time, but this was my subconscious giving her signals for help.

I would spend several late nights, writing depressing poetry. Sitting all alone, for hours at a time in the dark, I would become lost in my thoughts while listening to hope-zapping songs like 'Stairway to Heaven' repeatedly. I was really good at nurturing my pain.

LONELY

Written Friday, December 3rd, 1982 during Workspare

I am swallowed up in the depths of despair,
As far as I'm concerned, nobody will care.
My mood is ugly, dark and black,
My heart's irregular beating could trigger a heart attack.
My erratic breathing is deadly slow,
Around me a sinister light begins to glow.
I am too far gone to call for help,
It would be insane to act like a dog and yelp.
I do not move but blankly stare,
My eyes do not blink at the steady glare.
Leave me alone and let me ponder,
My mind and soul are left to wander.
You would not like to be near me in my present state,
For you would go under as well and meet your fate!

Julie vander Maden

Boy, how I wish I had read Josh McDowell's book "*More Than a Carpenter*" back then. In Josh's book, he challenges the reader to decide whether or not Jesus was a liar, a lunatic, or Lord after looking at historical evidence the same way we use evidence to decide a verdict in our courts today.

First, this means analyzing the body of evidence that has been passed down to us, which by the way, includes over 24,000 manuscripts of the Bible! The next largest collection of manuscripts is of Homer's "*Illiad*" at only 642 copies. And despite the fact that it is almost impossible to pass on informa-tion intact through a handful of people, it has been proven that these biblical manuscripts are over 99% accurate with only the odd spelling mistake or wrong pronoun usage. That is abso-lutely miraculous, as far as I am concerned.

Second, you must look at eyewitness accounts. The Bible has over 500 eyewitness accounts in just one public gath-ering alone. Pretty amazing. Not to mention another 40 days of Jesus visiting with people before ascending to heaven.

Third, you must look at sources of historical evidence out-side of the biblical texts. Josephus is well known and respected for his historical writings. He is a reliable third-party source as he was a non-Christian who favored Rome.

Josh suggests in *"More Than a Carpenter"* that if Jesus was a liar, would he die for a lie? I can't think of anyone that has knowingly died for a lie. Next, Josh suggests that if Jesus had convinced himself of his own lies, then Jesus would be considered a lunatic. But, it is difficult to look at all the wisdom that Jesus taught and say he was a lunatic. Only a person who fully believed what they were preaching to the point of going to their death for it could be considered a lunatic.

So, if the body of historical evidence agrees, eyewitness accounts agree, then Jesus could *not* be a liar, or a lunatic, or just a good teacher; he must be the Son of God. That is the conclusion that I have come to, but I, once again, strongly challenge you to read Josh McDowell's book "*More Than a Carpenter*", so that you can come to your own conclusions. I also strongly recommend Lee Strobel's book "*A Case For a Creator*". Lee presents scientific arguments for our universe being created by intelligent design. Both Josh and Lee are former atheists with powerful testimonies of how God turned their thinking around. Their writings have been very inspiring and enlightening to me over the years.

UNTITLED

Written in late August, 1982 while sitting on the garage roof of our house at sunset contemplating my existence.

As I look into the far distance
Where the treetops touch the clouds
The sun says its last good-night
With the bright pink rays reflected on the clouds
The air is warm and moist
As you hear the quiet buzzing of flying insects
In the rich, dewy grass
The crickets sing whole-heartedly
A soft, gentle breeze ripples through the leaves
Like a butterfly that gently flutters its wings
Gradually the azure sky transforms into an ebony blanket
With silver coins embedded throughout its entirety
How I wish I could listen all through the black night
To the grand orchestra of insects
And watch the stars sparkle in the endless sky
How small I am in this vast and mysterious place
As I look up into the sky
There seems to be no end to its existence.
It boggles the mind!

Julie vander Maden

But since I hadn't read Josh and Lee's books yet, I was left to figure things out on my own. I had several elderly relatives, so I was used to going to funerals, but nothing prepared me for losing someone young and full of life like Steve. I had grown close to Tom's family and Steve was dating Tom's older sister, Emily. Steve was tall, handsome, polite, smart and on the football team, but Steve battled throat cancer. Despite the horrible treatments, he was always up and smiling. He was a joy to be around, and now at barely 20 years old, I was going to his funeral. As far as I understand, Emily never married after Steve. I bundled up all the hurt and unanswered questions about why Steve had to die inside my already tortured mind and just left it there.

In grade ten I auditioned for the school play "*Teahouse of the August Moon*". I was 'over the moon' when I discovered that I had won the female lead of Lotus Blossom, a geisha girl. Our drama teacher, Ms Bean, had lived in Japan for two years, so she insisted that all the Japanese characters learn their lines in proper Japanese. I had to listen to my lines on cassette tape (I know, an ancient piece of technology) over and over until she was satisfied with my pronunciation. I didn't mind the challenge at all. In fact, I was really proud of my accomplishment. Because my role was a geisha girl, she even took me to Toronto to learn how to dance a proper geisha dance with fans at the Japanese cultural center. I learned how to walk and move with slow flowing movements just like a geisha girl. I practiced walking with my toes pointing inwards, and taking tiny steps in my tight kimono so much, that I even caught myself walking like that in the grocery store with my mother after rehearsal. I loved researching and becoming the character. I read up on lots of Japanese culture in order to gain a deeper understanding of my role. I even had to endure a hot, itchy geisha wig, but I didn't complain. Anything for the role.

I'LL ALWAYS REMEMBER YOU
(For the cast of "Teahouse of the August Moon")

Written March 18th, 1983 on the last night of the play.

As each day quickly passes by,
It gets harder to think and not start to cry.
For the time I have spent with all of you,
Has changed my days to "hoppee" from blue.
I know that all good things must finally end,
But at least I have each one of you as my friend.
Together, we can re-live the memories from the past,
And recall all the characters from our remarkable cast.

Our knowledge has grown from working so closely together,
And learning with you is what I treasure forever.
Because to me, you were teachers as well as peers,
Without knowing it, you comforted my hidden fears.

As you have heard me say before,
Saying "good-bye" is something I abhor.
Even though we must turn away and now depart,
The laughs, the jokes, the smiles, will always be in my heart.

Julie vander Maden

In the play, Lotus Blossom falls in love with an American soldier, but is not allowed to develop the relationship. Well, like so many actors out there, I started to fall for my leading man. I ended it with Tom, which was horrible. He was such a sweet guy, but he didn't care about theater or the arts, or traveling. He was a tobacco farmer who loved hockey and staying home. Tom was also leaving for an agricultural college in the fall, and my dad had made it clear that he wanted our relationship to end. My father thought we were way too serious for our age. Dan, who played opposite me, was more goofy than Tom, but he loved theater. He had a deep, rich singing voice, and he played, and wrote, his own classical music on the piano. His talent swept me off my feet. His mother was even a former finalist in the 1953 Miss Canada pageant. She was such a beautiful woman inside and out. Our relationship didn't last long though. For all his talent, he was still a little too goofy for me. That June, for a brief moment, I was without a boyfriend – something I didn't like to experience.

That's when a whole new door opened up for me. I found something else that I could be 'good at'. My mother's girlfriend started pushing me to enter the Strathroy Turkey Festival pageant. It became a joke. I had no intention of being called a Turkey Queen. There were some nice prizes though, so at the last minute I entered the pageant.

Now I know what you are thinking, "What in the world is a Turkey Festival?" Well, in Strathroy, Cuddy Farms is a huge local business. They raise turkey and chickens. At the time, I was told that the company was responsible for supplying the chicken for Russia's McDonalds. At least, that was what

I was told. In any case, Cuddy Farms was the 'big cheese' at the time, hence Strathroy has a Turkey Festival even to this day. Ironically, they no longer choose a Turkey Queen. For a while they even changed the name to 'Festival Queen'. I do not know why the pageant no longer exists, but I suspect that there are not *too* many girls out there who want to be associated with a turkey.

All the contestants attended a luncheon to meet with the judges before pageant night. At the pageant we were to walk, introduce ourselves, recite a memorized speech and then answer an impromptu question. Well, before I tell you how it all turned out, let me tell you the challenge I had in just arriving in time to compete.

"What time is it?" I yelled from the bathroom.

"You have about an hour before we have to go," my mother replied.

"Ok, hair and makeup, here we go," I thought to myself.

Finally it was time to put on my new, turquoise sundress with white trim. I was so excited to wear it.

"Mom, could you help me do up my zipper?"

"Ok, just hang on."

ZIP. "Wait a minute. That didn't sound right." My mind began to race.

Panicking, my mother exclaimed, "The zipper broke!"

"What? Are you kidding me? What are we going to do? Can you fix it? I don't have anything else to wear. I can't wear the same dress that I wore at the luncheon to the pageant! Not to mention I have to leave in just a few minutes! Mom, what can we do?"

"Hang on, hang on. I can't fix the zipper. The only thing I can do is sew you into the dress."

"Sew me into the dress? You mean stand here while you take a needle and thread and sew me up?"

"That's what I mean. Do you want me to or not?"

"Ok, ok, do it. I don't have any other choice. I just hope you can sew fast. I'm going to be late!"

Here I was all dolled up, leaning forward with my dress hiked up, while my precious mother proceeded to sew like lightning and try not to poke me with the needle. I attempted to rehearse my speech, but my head was swirling with thoughts of disaster. I could hardly remember a word of what I prepared to say.

Finally she finished and we all grabbed our things as we ran out the door. Time was of the essence. So much for peace and composure.

We raced to Alexandra Park where the Turkey Festival was being held. I walked as quickly as possible in my high heels without trying to break a sweat (remember it was the end of June) because the last thing I wanted was to look undignified and sweaty. A flat bed truck was the stage and the contestants were waiting in the trailer. I was the last one to arrive and they had wondered if I was coming at all. *Not* a good way to start my first beauty pageant by any stretch of the imagination.

I took more deep breaths and I tried to forget all the chaos I had gone through just to get there in time. Things went pretty smoothly until it can time for my speech. About one third of the way into my speech, I went *totally* blank. Just like that, I stopped speaking and my mind raced over the speech again to find my place. At the same time, I knew that I had to make it look like all was well, that I had it under control, so I continued to smile around the crowd. After what seemed like eternity, my speech popped back into my head and I finished with ease. I walked backstage and thought to myself what a disaster I had made. Kiss those prizes good-bye. I just made a fool of myself.

Once the previous year's Turkey Festival Queen took her traditional farewell walk, it was time to crown the new queen. After my fiasco, I didn't have a lot of interest in hearing the results. Third, second, and first runner-ups were called, and of course, I wasn't one of them. Finally they announced the winner. Did I hear right? That sounded like *my* name, but how could it be? The pageant host smiled and turned to me. I *wasn't* hearing things. I won!

The rest of the festival weekend involved riding in an antique convertible for the parade, awarding people with event prizes, being forced into the dunk tank, and being kissed by way too many sweaty 5km runners. Yuck. Despite the sweaty kisses, it was a fun time. The only awkward moment I had was shortly after all the pageant photos and interviews. You see, although I was technically unattached, both Tom and Dan came to con-gratulate me. They both stood about 15 feet apart, waiting their turn to hug me. I felt so bad for them. They still wanted me back even though I caused them both such heartache.

After the festival finished, I was off to start another adven-ture. I had auditioned for the Huron County Playhouse's summer theatre. This was professional theater, even though I wouldn't get paid as a high school student. I received the role of one of the blind girls in "*The Miracle Worker*". It was an eye-opening experience. In only three weeks rehearsal, these professional actors were ready to perform, while it took us months of rehearsal for our school plays. I loved the intensity of the theater. I enjoyed the challenge of preparing to act like I was born blind.

After the production's run, things slowed down and I wanted to make some summer money. I hated babysitting, but there didn't seem to be any other option available to me. I was hired to babysit for a woman who worked at the same hospital as my mother. The thought of taking care of a baby boy and his toddler sister all day made me depressed. I really loathed babysitting. I wanted to do something more exciting.

To my surprise, I received an interesting phone call just a couple days after starting my babysitting job. It was Joe Bernard. He was one of my judges at the Strathroy Turkey Festival pageant. What I didn't know was that he owned the higher end shoe store in town. After getting reacquainted on the phone, he proceeded to ask me if I would be interested in a part-time job at his shoe store. I couldn't believe my ears. I was actually being sought out for a job. No interview – just, do you want it? Before I got too excited, I had to tell Joe that I wasn't sixteen yet, the legal age to work part-time. He asked me when my birthday was and I told him it was in September. "No problem, I will have you start doing small, odd jobs for a lower wage until I can hire you properly after your birthday," he said. Awesome. I gave the woman I just started babysitting for two weeks to find a replacement. Then I was off to my new job as a shoe salesmen.

It was the beginning of a 3 1/2 year career working for Joe, and I couldn't have had a nicer boss. Once I began working for him, I asked him, "Why, in the world would you call me out-of-the blue for a job?" I was shocked to hear his response. It all had to do with the Strathroy Turkey Festival pageant. When he saw how I blanked out during my speech and yet, managed to maintain complete composure, he knew I was the kind of employee he wanted in his store. Incredible. Here I thought I had made a complete mess of the pageant, and I ended up receiving *two* major blessings – the reigning title *and* a new job.

I have to say, I was never very good at selling shoes. On several occasions, I would ask Joe, "Why do you keep me? I guess I am just good advertisement for the store because of the pageants." He always kept my pageant pictures up by the cash register for the customers to see. At least I was good for something.

I love looking back at this time in my life and seeing how God used my failures to bring about some amazing successes. We are so afraid to fail today in our society. I have heard that some sports clubs give everyone a ribbon or trophy even if they were the worst team or player. How do we learn any life lessons from that kind of treatment? Life *promises* to knock us down sometimes, and if we don't learn how to overcome obstacles we will never learn what determination, persistence and tenacity really mean. True success comes with a price. It's true that we never really value something unless our own sweat and blood goes towards obtaining it. I could have bowed out of the pageant because I did not have another dress to wear, but I didn't. I could have walked off the stage when I went blank during my speech because of all the stress I went through just trying to get there in time, but I didn't give up. I hung in there and tried my best anyway – and guess what – God showed up. I won the pageant and I got a job on top of it, all because one of the judges was so impressed with my perseverance. How cool is that? You never know what God will do with your failures, if you will only do your part and never ever give up on yourself.

A famous quote from Thomas Edison who invented the light bulb is, "Results? Why, man, I have gotten lots of results! If I find 10,000 ways something won't work, I haven't failed. I am not discouraged, because every wrong attempt discarded is often a step forward..."

It is important to understand what our personal motivation is for success, too. Unfortunately, I was a hyper –achiever because I lacked the understanding of who I really was in God's eyes. I was motivated by my own insecurities and need for acceptance instead of by God's love and desire to see me flourish in His plan for my life. I did everything in my own strength. My successes and failures were all my own. What is really cool is how God intervened in my circumstances even though my motivation was misdirected. I could have just given it all I had and still lost the pageant and never got the job, but God showed me how He can work through people to bring about success *His* way.

So when you understand who you are in God, that nothing happens without a reason, and you add these truths to your own unwavering resolve and determination to give your best at everything you do, God *will* show up in amazing and unpredictable ways in your life – despite your successes or failures.

Psalm 37:23,24 "The steps of a man are established by the Lord, and He delights in his way. When he falls, he will not be hurled headlong, because the Lord is the One who holds his hand."

MOMENTS OF REFLECTION

Have you solidified your own convictions about the authenticity of the Bible and Christ's existence as the Son of God?

Do you have dominating insecurities in your life that influence your decision- making?

Have you questioned what drives you? Is it to please God or your own desire to succeed for personal gain?

Are you able to see any areas in your life that are unhealthy because you are making the decisions instead of God leading you?

Have you struggled with eating disorders, or at least with very unhealthy eating habits?

Have you asked yourself why you focus on food so much? There is always an underlying reason why people turn to eating disorders. The eating disorder is only a manifestation of some- thing more serious going on emotionally, or psychologically.

Please see the section at the back of the book for more information on eating disorders.

Chapter Five

THE DATE-RAPE NIGHTMARE

"You're so beautiful. I've never felt like this with anyone else before. I'll never leave you. I don't care what you want to do in life; I'll follow wherever you go. I'll move to be near you at whatever university you choose. No one is ever going to take you away from me. You're mine now – forever."

Each word Bruce uttered was another loop latching itself onto the invisible chain being wrapped around my soul.

"What have I gotten myself into?" This can't be happening. This can't be. Say something. Say you don't want to be with him. Say you don't remember everything that happened last night. Say that you never ever meant for things to be more than casual dating. Break it off! Tell him to take you home and that this is *not* going any further. For heaven's sake, say *something!*"

But I couldn't seem to utter a single word that was whirling around in my head. My heart was pounding. I could hear the cheers of football fans coming from the TV. I looked around at his modest living-room and I thought to myself, "Is this it? Is this going to be my life? Has freewill been taken away from me?

How do I get out of here? We're all alone. What if he gets angry and refuses to drive me home. How will he react?"

I felt paralyzed by fear as the game continued to roar on in the background.

"Also, what about my reputation? What if he tells people what happened – even though I didn't *want* it to happen, and even though I don't remember much of *anything* that happened! What will people think of me? What will my parents think? How can I live with myself if the truth ever gets out? No, it can't get out. I have to hide it. I have to endure this. I have to accept my fate. It's obviously my fault."

It wasn't long after grade ten began that I got another boy-friend. This guy was cool. Sam wore camo, and had the latest haircut. He was a bit of a rebel, but he also had brains. He chased me hard, but his fire didn't last long. Before I knew it, it was my turn to be dumped – and I couldn't handle it. He dumped me by simply ignoring me. He tried to treat me badly without giving any explanation, so that I would just go away.

UNTITLED
Written in the fall of 1983 about Sam

Now you smile down at my face
But are its roots genuine?
Behind your eyes I search in the space
Searching for a meaningful solution
A mystifying sensation sends me tremors
I fight to remain tranquil
Yet my ears oddly have not heard rumors

I feel like a cold outsider
Your treatment seems cruel and unjust
Are you trying to donate a HINT??

Julie vander Maden

The worst episode happened when Sam invited me over for dinner at his house with his family. He picked me up and barely spoke to me during the car ride over to his house. After dinner he disappeared upstairs to his bedroom and never returned. I was left to visit with his parents and younger brother until I finally asked for a ride home. Sam never said he was upset or angry with me. He purely set out to quietly reject me. His younger brother apologized for his brother's bad behavior many times, but that didn't heal my heart. I had never experienced such intentional rejection before. I immediately spiraled into depression as my heart screamed for love.

UNTITLED
Written November 1983 after I finally confronted Sam about his ill treatment towards me.

I need someone to make me forget
All the fun we had together.
And the first time we ever met
To make it in the past forever.
I can't go on like this any longer
I wish someone would make me stronger
And create another spark.

Because I'm slowly dying
In my own lonely despair.
I've long stopped from trying
I can't seem to get anywhere.
So, will someone please help me?
I'm reaching out for you
Set my heart finally free
And show me what true love can do!

Julie vander Maden

During that same time period, I had another great opportunity. I was asked to sing for Prime Minister Pierre Elliott Trudeau. He was going to visit my town during his campaign for re-election and use our high school. I decided to sing a Broadway musical song from '*Kiss Me Kate*' by Samuel and Bella Spewack called '*I'm a Maid Who Would Marry any Tom, Dick or Harry*' written by Cole Porter. I sang it with three of my male drama friends. We had a lot of fun performing it. The guys insisted that I should fall sideways into their arms, so that they could carry me off stage still singing. It was cool. Afterwards, I was introduced to the Prime Minister. He complimented me on the performance and then took me by surprise by his following comment.

Prime Minister Trudeau said, "I wish *my* name was Tom, Dick or Harry."

Yikes, he was in his early sixties at the time, and I was barely sixteen. That was not the kind of the attention I was looking for.

But, I was desperately looking for another guy to fill the hole in my heart. I needed to have male attention and approval all the time. Like so many young girls, if they don't have a strong bond with their father, they will try to bond with another male. That was me. Going a weekend without a date was a disastrous thought in my eyes. Unfortunately, I was getting quite a lot of attention from a 21 year old. He returned to high school as a mature student to complete his grade twelve diploma. Bruce would pop into the shoe store frequently to say hi. Tam, one of the other young, female employees, could see that he liked me, and she began to tease me about him. Even my boss, Joe, pushed me to go out with him. The truth was that I was not interested in him at all. I certainly didn't find him attractive, but after having my heart crushed by Sam, and no other dates coming around the corner, I finally said yes to go on a date. When I think back, I can't believe that my parents allowed a sixteen year old to go out with a 21 year old, but they probably didn't want to fight with me. Besides, he came from a nice family.

After two dates, Bruce wanted a more serious relationship. It was evident how taken he was with me. I needed the attention, but something about him made me feel uneasy. I brushed it off as just our age difference, but I wish I had given more heed to my inner voice. Clearly that was the Holy Spirit trying to speak to me, but I ignored it. There was a wild look in his dark brown eyes that made my skin crawl, but I was so desperate to not feel alone and rejected, that I accepted his attention anyway. I tried to get over how much I disliked his kisses. I wished so much that someone else had pursued me, but I didn't want any time to pass. Feeling cherished to someone was such an overwhelming drive within me that every negative aspect had to be overlooked. Nothing else mattered, even if I didn't find a single thing attractive about him.

Then the inevitable happened. I remember it so clearly. On Friday night we were sitting in his apartment and everything within me wanted to scream *no*. Bruce wanted to make our involvement official. He asked me to go steady with him in so many words. I had stopped going to my church after I was confirmed at fourteen, but I still prayed every night. I know now that the Holy Spirit was warning me not to make the wrong decision, but incredibly, my starving heart needed to be adored by somebody at all costs. I bitterly regretted saying the word 'yes' as it was coming out of my mouth. I immediately felt like something died in me. It felt like a cloud of darkness descended upon my soul – and it had.

Saturday morning my family and I traveled to Toronto for the Royal Winter Fair where I fulfilled my duty as the reigning Turkey Festival Queen. My job was to stand at the Cuddy Farms' booth and hand out turkey sausage tasters. I enjoyed meeting the public, but that whole weekend I kept thinking about the horrific decision I made to be Bruce's girlfriend. I tried to think of any nice way to back out of it, but I couldn't think of anything. I felt completely trapped. I had fallen into my own pit. I felt my life was over.

Christmas time had arrived and the party season began. Joe, held a lovely dinner party for all his staff – on December 10th, 1983, a date I can never forget. I had brought Bruce as my guest. I don't remember much about the evening, but one thing I do remember is that my wine glass was never empty. Yes, I was drinking alcohol underage. It wasn't the first time. Since I was thirteen, I was experimenting with alcohol. Every party had alcohol. It was normal. But this night, Bruce was very attentive to my wine glass. He made sure that I never had an empty glass. Now, I was stick thin and anorexic, so it wouldn't take much of anything to get me drunk.

I vaguely remember the drive home and trying to say good-night to Bruce in his car. My parents were staying overnight somewhere else for a Christmas party and my brother, Norm, was at a friend's house. I was going to be alone in the house all night. I remember Bruce wanting to come into the house. I tried to stop him. I was feeling sick from the alcohol. My memory only has bits and pieces after that. I remember a flash of him on top of me on the couch. Then it was morning. He hadn't stayed the night. I don't know when he left, but I was glad he was gone. I was so drunk.

That afternoon he wanted me to come over and watch football. I hate watching televised football, just like I hate watching televised hockey, but he picked me up in his car anyway. He started saying some things about the night before, and the reality of what happened began to sink in. I had been date-raped. Now he thought he had full access to me at any time. My life was over. I blamed myself completely.

Later that day, my mom called to tell me to come home. She was very upset with me because apparently I threw up beside the toilet – and the vomit was still there. I was so drunk that I had absolutely no recollection of it ever happening. I was mortified and ashamed to face my parents about getting drunk, never mind everything else that was swirling in my mind over Bruce!

I couldn't tell a soul what had happened. I pretended that everything was fine, but everything was *far* from fine. By Christmas day, just **two weeks** after the rape, I had gained 25 lbs. That's how *fine* I was. I turned to my precious eating disorder and I binged like there was no tomorrow. It was my transition from anorexia to both anorexia/bulimia (starving and binging/purging cycles). My mother had bought me a pair of black dress pants for Christmas, but they didn't fit on Christmas day. Baggy palozza pants were in fashion at the time, so I wore my black palozza pants all the time. Nothing else fit. Festivities abounded around me while I was spiraling down into my own abyss.

Bruce kept talking about how we would always be together and that he would follow me anywhere. I was interested in possibly applying for the Theater program at York University in Toronto and, of course, Bruce said he would move there with me in a heartbeat. The thought made me nauseous. The situation seemed completely hopeless to me. He became very possessive. I didn't know how I could get out of the mess that *I had caused* in the first place, so I stayed. I acted the lead part in my own tragic play. He never knew how scared I was of him. He thought it was consensual. I told him repeatedly that I didn't want to have sex and he would stop pressuring me for a little while, but it never lasted. I was living my own nightmare. During each episode, I used to pretend that he was someone else that I liked, so it didn't seem so bad. He even nicknamed me 'Alkie" because I always drank when I was with him. Anything to dull my senses, to imagine someone else, and to make the performance easier was all I could think about. It took me nine months to find a way to escape from him. The sad part is that my parents were never happy about the relationship. They wanted it to end, but I felt like I couldn't tell them what happened because I blamed myself for the rape. I was so incredibly ashamed. Instead, I ended up defending Bruce to my parents when I really wanted to scream to them, "Rescue you me!!"

There were instances where other girls said how lucky I was to have him as a boyfriend, and how much they would like to go out with him. I would reply, "Go for it! I don't want him." They would be shocked and confused as to why I didn't want him.

Even my best friend, who didn't know the whole story about us, asked me if I thought that I would marry him. I replied, "Definitely not!" She also wondered why I responded so harshly and with such finality. If she only knew.

UNTITLED
Written near the end of June 1984 in my first attempt to creatively express 'the need' to break up without stirring his anger. I was always 'acting' the part of the loving girlfriend. I never gave him the poem.

I saw a movie the other day
There was a role that I must play
It isn't the first time I've played the part
Believe me, I know if off by heart.

The movie star was sorrowful and sad
But not because her love had turned bad
Their lives had taken different directions
Separating their love and affections.

Unwillingly they were forced to part
Each having left with a broken heart.
I cried when the movie was done
Because I knew she wasn't the only one
I, too, am sorrowful and pained
Because I, too, am left alone once again.

Julie vander Maden

MOMENTS OF REFLECTION

Have you or anyone close to you suffered from sexual abuse?

Did you report it to the police, or at least to a parent, friend or relative?

If yes, were you believed? What steps were taken to begin the healing process?

If no, why not? How did you cope after the experience? Do you have someone close to you now that you trust to share your experience with? Have you looked into speaking with a pastor, youth pastor, counselor, or at least reading a book on sexual abuse recovery? Keeping it a secret only cripples your own life. God can heal you, but the first step is to open up about the experience.

Sometimes writing a letter to the offender, that you never intend to send, can be therapeutic. Share your feelings in the letter unapologetically.

Just remember, that if you are serious about getting your life back, you must choose to forgive your offender, at some point. Not for his sake, but yours. Don't allow him to unknowingly continue to hurt you by forever living in the past. Forgiveness frees you. It shows that he no longer has a hold on your present or future life.

I found this next step to be the hardest for me, but you have to forgive yourself. If God can forgive us all of our sins, then who are we to not forgive ourselves? Are we bigger than God? Obviously, we are not!

Chapter Six

BEAUTY PAGEANTS – A REASON TO LIVE

E ven though I wouldn't say that I am a great promoter of pageants, I certainly have to admit that entering pageants kept me alive. Each competition gave me a goal to reach, something to work towards. And thankfully, right after New Year's Day, I entered the Miss Teen London pageant. I immediately started dieting like crazy and I even exercised at home. Remember, I didn't take gym class in high school. I managed to lose the 25 lbs in time before my first interview.

Things went much smoother at the Miss Teen London interview, but still not without a little hiccup. After answering several questions from the judges, I was asked to take a walk for them. This should have been a piece of cake, but I actually had to concentrate on walking gracefully. I had grabbed my dress shoes from work, but I didn't realize that I took one of my shoes and one of Tam's shoes. We owned the same style, but not the same size. I wore a half size larger than her because I have wider feet. My one foot felt so pinched and crammed that I wanted to limp the whole time, but that wouldn't look very graceful. Once again, I used shear determination to put on a good show and glide in front of them.

It wasn't long before I received the news that I had made it as a semi-finalist. I was to be part of the live contest to be held at White Oaks Mall in London. We rehearsed a couple times for the show and I got to see what kind of competition I was up against. One girl, Susan, had won 1st Runner –up the year before and she had lots of professional modeling experience. She seemed to be quite favored by the support staff. In fact, everyone had taken modeling except me. One of the judges referred to me as the 'Natural'. He thought I carried myself well, despite the fact that I hadn't received any formal training. I certainly felt intimidated though. I always felt like the underdog.

Pageant night was both nerve-racking and exciting. A huge crowd had gathered to watch. Once again, I had a little hiccup to deal with. When I walked out modeling my first outfit, the scarf they gave me to wear started to slip off. Instead of tripping on it, I grabbed it and purposely threw it off stage. Might as well make it look like it was supposed to happen.

In the end, Susan, who won 1st Runner-up the year before, was crowned Miss Teen London 1984. But, I managed to win 1st Runner-up. Not bad. Not bad at all. My parents were thrilled. Of course, Bruce came to watch me. He said that he wanted to ride on my shirt-tales to fame. That terrified me. That did not help with an exit strategy.

After the pageant, I was able to throw myself into more theater. Our high school wasn't doing a large production that year, but Ms Bean, our drama teacher, decided to do a French play entitled, *"La Leçon"*(The Lesson). It was a psychological thriller about a crazy professor who ends up killing his student. I was the student. The play only had two characters in it, with a brief, third character at the very end. *And* it was to be performed completely in French. Now, I was taking honor's level French in high school, but I was really weak at conversational French. It was a great challenge to memorize all the lines. The most difficult challenge was trying to improvise in French. My friend, Alvin, who played the professor, had the bulk of the lines, and would frequently lose his place. I had to try to help him find his way back – in French. It was scary, to say the least. We had to perform for all the French classes in the whole school district, so most of them would know if we messed up.

The irony was that I played a bubbly, out-going student who tried her hardest to achieve success in order to please the professor. Initially pleasant, the professor quickly shows his true colors and begins to break her spirit and eventually murders her. In some ways, it mirrored my own life, as I was slowly dying in my bondage to Bruce.

Once *'La Lecon'* was done, it was back to normal school life. Bruce continued to dream up plans for my future, which, of course, included him tagging along. He repeatedly told me that wherever I went, he would follow. His words were like a noose that was slowly being tightened around my neck.

I continued to sway between starving myself and then binging. My favored way of purging was to stick a finger down my throat. I have always had a super sensitive gag reflex, but it is amazing how performing an action repeatedly can wear down a person's sensitivity. Eventually, I had to work my way up to three fingers down my throat, before I could finally gag.

What I didn't realize was that my face was not getting fat, but rather bloated from all the stomach acid passing through my mouth. I had not idea what kind of damage I was causing my developing body through starving and purging. Time would eventually catch up with me.

MOMENTS OF REFLECTION:

Has there been some situation, or event, or person that has helped distract, or deter you from making more unhealthy decisions?

Can you look back and see how God may have tried to steer you out of a bad situation?

Have you ever felt 'stuck' in a situation and unable to figure a way out?

Where, or who have you turned to in those cases?

How did you choose to deal with it?

Did you run to God, your Strong Tower, or did you try to manage it on your own?

Did you think to pray about the situation? When? Immediately or after you tried everything else?

Chapter Seven

THE MATCHMAKER

With summer around the corner, I searched for another community production to audition in. I won the role of Minnie Fay in "*The Matchmaker*". It was a high school community production to be performed at the London Community Theater. I was looking forward to working with other actors from different schools. Bruce was not so keen on the idea. He warned me that I better not get involved with anyone in the play. He was very jealous.

In the script I read that my character, Minnie Fay, was to be kissed by the character, Barnaby Tucker. I was very curious to find out just what the actor playing Barnaby Tucker looked like. On the first day of rehearsal, I was not disappointed. James was 6'1" with dark brown hair and dark brown eyes. All the girls seemed to be buzzing around him. I definitely didn't want Bruce to meet James.

It was a crazy summer. Bruce would drive me to my rehearsal in London on some days, and I would spend the day falling deeper under James' spell. I discovered that James was a top grade student who played the saxophone, piano and sang with a soft, smooth velvety voice. I quickly found myself spending more time after rehearsals hanging out with the cast. Several of us hit it off well. We would go to someone's house, and meet at restaurants, but our favorite hangout was a piano bar. Every single one of us was still under age, but we all got served. We loved this place because anyone could get up and perform a Broadway musical song. I made sure that Bruce never joined me on any of these outings. The closer I got to James, the more I hoped he would be able to rescue me from Bruce.

By the end of the summer, James and I were definitely an item. Now we had to figure out how to get me away from Bruce. James did not have the backbone I hoped for, so he was afraid of any negative aftermath from Bruce. James didn't want Bruce to know anything about him.

HIDE INSIDE WITHOUT HELP

Written August 29th 1984 before I got the courage to speak to Bruce about ending our relationship without telling him about James.

What am I to do?
My mind is in a constant turmoil
I think of nothing else.
My mood is disguised for public eyes
No one should know the truth.
I hide my frustrations inside –
They must not show on me.

I debate within my weary head
But wide awake I look.
My heavy heart drags through all of this.
When can I lie and rest?
No one believes the dreaded task I face.
They won't see my side.
They won't try to help.

Julie vander Maden

I decided to use my parents as a reason to break up, which was definitely legitimate. The truth was they never wanted me together with Bruce in the first place. On Labor Day weekend, the beginning of grade eleven, I told Bruce that my parents were forcing me to break it off with him. He was furious. Thankfully, Bruce had finished his grade twelve, so he was off to college in London. At least he wouldn't be at my high school any more, or around the store very often.

I thought I was finally free of him. I began to relax a little. James lived in London, so we could only see each other on the weekends, and have late night phone calls. He continued to worship the ground I walked on. Even his parents said that they had never seen him so smitten before. He had never had a girl-friend for more than two months. On my birthday in September, he presented me with a promise ring. It had a little blue sap-phire (my birth stone) surrounded by four little diamond chips. I was shocked. It was small, but I loved it. James only worked part-time at a convenience store, so he got a great deal from his brother's jewelry store. He was really serious about our relationship lasting the long haul.

Later that fall, I found out that I had won the acting award for my performance in *'La Lecon'*. Even though I was only in grade eleven, the school wished to present me with the award at their annual commencement for graduates. I really appreciated the honor and I looked forward to inviting James to attend with me.

It started off as a great night. I wore my best dress. I bought 4" high heel pumps from my store, so that I would be a little closer to James in height. It was great to have him on my arm as we sat down together. I couldn't be happier – until I saw Bruce. He was also there to receive his grade twelve diploma. It had been over two months since we had officially broken up, but this was the first time he was seeing me with another guy. Bruce may have been sitting on the other side of the auditorium, but if looks could kill, James would have been dead instantly. Bruce obviously recognized James from the seeing him in the summer production. I received my award and returned to my seat. Then they started to hand out diplomas. I knew things were going from bad to worse, when I saw how Bruce snatched his diploma without even a hint of a smile. He had a look of fierce determination on his face, as he shot his gaze down at us from the stage.

I never said a word to my parents that I had concerns about Bruce. After commencement, they were headed home, and James and I were supposed to go to one of the after parties. As we said goodnight to my parents, I caught a glimpse of Bruce. He was glaring at us like a lion waiting to attack his prey. I suggested to James that maybe we should try to slip out a different exit, so that we wouldn't collide with Bruce. We tried to make sure that he didn't see us, but it wasn't easy. We walked as quickly as possible down the empty hall. The exit door was in sight and no one was following us. We were almost home free. As we walked out the doors, I caught my breath for a second. Then, wham! Bruce came running full tilt around the building and plowed James to the ground. He was yelling and swearing and threatening to kill James as he was trying to pound his face. James refused to fight back. Instead he tried to deflect Bruce's punches with his arms. In my most expensive dress, and 4" leather high heels, I threw myself on top of Bruce and exerted every bit of strength I had to try and pull Bruce off of James. As the three of us were sliding down the grassy hillside of the school, I saw several people walking to their cars. I screamed and screamed for help, and every single one of them got into their cars and drove away without a second look. As we reached the bottom of the hill, I pried Bruce off of James and told him to run. I wrapped my arms and one leg around Bruce as he shouted obscenities and death threats constantly at James.

"I'll kill you! I'll kill you! She's mine!"

"Stop it! Just leave us alone! Stop it! I don' t want to have anything to do with you!" I continued screaming at Bruce, desperate for him to just walk away.

"I promise, I will kill you if you show up at that party. I mean it. You're dead. Don't even think of showing up. I promise you, I'll kill you!" Bruce repeatedly threatened James before he finally relented. An inch from his face, I felt his heavy breathing, the tenseness of all his muscles and the pounding of his heart against my chest. Glaring at me like a wild animal, I tentatively began to peel myself off of him. He threw out a few more obscenities and threats as he began to back away.

James and I quickly fumbled our way to the car. Our nice clothes were covered in dirt and grass stains. I was surprised that I hadn't broken a heel. We tried to calm each other down as we drove the five minutes back to my house. My whole body was shaking. I thought I was starting to calm down as we approached my house, until I tried to step out of the car. I took a couple steps, and then I collapsed on my front lawn. James rushed over to me and cradled me in his arms. I shook uncontrollably and started to hyperventilate. Then I started screaming in between each hyperventilated breath. My parents heard the screams and ran outside. I don't know how long it took for them to calm me down, but eventually they were able to bring me inside.

We all sat around the dining-room table and retold the night's events to my parents. James was visibly shaken, scared and bruised, but at least nothing was broken. We didn't know if we should go to the police. I was scared of more retaliation from Bruce. One thing was for sure, neither one of us was going to dare step a foot at that party.

James left for home after breakfast. He was no longer his joyful self. He seemed really eager to get out of Strathroy as fast as he could. In the back of my mind, I hoped this wouldn't ruin our relationship.

My body was in total pain. I couldn't believe how much every muscle in my body hurt. It was as if I just went through a horrific car accident. My body was completely traumatized. It took almost two weeks for me to physically recover.

What I didn't realize at the time is that this seemed to set the stage for the development of my mysterious aches and pains in my joints and muscles. It would be several years later before I could finally put a name on my condition – fibromyalgia.

After James left, I pulled out every gift Bruce had every given me. My father loved to burn old brush beside the weeping willow tree, so I took the clothing and other gifts out to be burned. Bruce had also given me several pieces of gold jewelry. I put them in an envelope and mailed it back to him. When I look back I think to myself, "Why didn't you just sell the jewelry, you stupid girl." But I didn't care, I just had to erase every single thing from my life that he had given or touched. The burning was like a cleansing ritual, I guess. I wanted to regain some power in my life. The thought of going around town, and running into Bruce, simply terrified the life out of me. I knew that just going to work would increase my chances of seeing him because he had family living near the shoe store. I had waited so long to be released from his control over my life and now I felt he was taking it back again.

"Aw, there he is!" I could feel my heart leap within my chest as if someone had just stabbed me.

"He must *not* see me. Oh pleassssse don't turn and see me." I could hardly catch a breath as my heart continued to pound against my ribcage.

"Hang onto the steering wheel, you fool." My hands were clammy and shaking so badly that I could barely steer the car. I felt like I was going to vomit and pass out at any second.

"Crap! He's looking at me. You just stay away. Don't even think of coming up to the car." Bruce shot daggers at me before very slowly turning away.

I parked, turned off the ignition, and collapsed into my seat. "I can't live like this. How dare he have this kind of grip on my life." I waited for my body to stop shaking before leaving the car and entering the back door to the shoe store.

Unfortunately, living in a small town makes it rather difficult to *not* run into people, so I had to endure several scary moments like this one. At least Bruce never approached me again. He just threatened me with his dark, piercing eyes. For years I would have a panic attack every time I thought I saw him, even if it turned out that it wasn't him after all. I would have to pause, catch my breath, wait for my heart to stop pounding and for my body to stop shaking uncontrollably.

The next day after Bruce's attack on us, my parents spoke to a lawyer about the situation. He said that if we were not pressing charges than probably the only thing we could do was to put a restraining order on Bruce. I was afraid to do that because I didn't think any authority would be there in time to reinforce the restraining order if Bruce decided to show up to do something else. I decided to just be on the lookout at all times. James hardly came to Strathroy after that. I had to meet him in London instead. James was definitely a lover not a fighter, and he was scared.

I WEEP, I SOB, I CRY FOR ME

Written November 25th, 1984 – after Bruce's attack on James and me at my high school commencement.

I weep, I sob, I cry for me
And as I cry, I think of why I do.
I think of the past, present and future
And sometimes when the present looks bleak
All hope for the future vanishes.

I weep, I sob, I cry for me
And as I cry, I begin to hate.
I hate my sad and sinking spirits
And self-pity begins to flourish.
My hatred challenges my pity.

I weep, I sob, I cry for me
And as I cry, I think of you.
I think of the love that I keep inside
And I wish you could sometime see
That you're the only one there will ever be.

I weep, I sob, I cry for me
What will ever happen to me?

Julie vander Maden

By January, James had had enough. I am sure there was more than one reason why he decided to end our relationship.

After all, I was the longest girlfriend he had had up to that point. Could I really expect anything different from a 17 year old? He certainly wasn't getting all of me , that's for sure. But I also know that James dreaded coming to Strathroy after Bruce's attack. James was not a tough guy and he had no backbone when it came to this kind of thing.

It was a horrible break up. We had talked about a future together, with a promise ring and everything. He told me I was different from all the other girls, that we would last forever, etc., etc. You know the kind of things people say.

ONCE THERE WERE TWO PEOPLE
Written on Sunday, January 20th, 1985 after James broke up with me.

Once upon a time there were two.
People who many others knew.
And t'was during the summer when,
Friendship had grown from each of them.

But the friendship began to grow,
And the feelings began to show.
Their friendship turned to love,
And together they soared high above.

Together they laughed and joked and shared,
So it seemed that their love had been spared,
From factors that had been staked,
As temptation for them to break.

At the end, temptation got its way,
And the one love went astray.
His love was dead and gone,
But she couldn't stop holding on.

He asked for friendship once again,
To be friends like way back when.
So what could she do but try,
Because she could never say good-bye.

Julie vander Maden

I was staying in London at a close friend's place for the weekend when James broke up with me. I was a complete mess. James was my 'knight in shining armor' who had rescued me out of Bruce's clutches. Now, not even he wanted me. That night I drowned myself in alcohol and blubbered all over my friend. I remember she suggested that we should go out for some fresh air, even though it was close to midnight, and the middle of January. I threw all self-respect to the wind as I was crying and yelling at cars, and stumbling down the snow-packed sidewalk while my friend tried to hold me up. I had hit rock bottom again.

MOMENTS OF REFLECTION:

Have you ever tried to lead a double life like I did with Bruce and James? Did you find it complicated to keep the secrets straight? When God is in control, there is no need for secrets, just freedom in his perfect truth.

I had to learn the hard way that people will always let you down. I should have gone to Jesus with all my needs, but instead I let myself be set up for more heartbreak. Can you think of a time where you have been stubborn and full of your own self-will that led you into pain and suffering?

Is Jesus your 'Knight in shining armor'? Deuteronomy 31:8 says, "The LORD himself goes before you and will be with you; he will never leave you nor forsake you. Do not be afraid; do not be discouraged."

Chapter Eight

REACHING FOR THE PRIZE

O nce again, a beauty pageant saved me. At the beginning of January, before James broke up with me, I had
already entered the Miss Teen London 1985 beauty pageant.
I figured that since I was so close to winning the year before, I
might as well give it another shot–all part of my hyper-achiever
syndrome. I breezed through my first interview to be accepted
as a semi-finalist. Fortunately, the judge who had called me
'the Natural' the previous year was once again judging the pageant. In preparation for the contest, I exercised at home, and
fasted more than binging in order to keep my weight down.

I put all my hope and focus into the pageant. It was the only,
less destructive way, I could deal with my broken heart. I even
risked losing the lead role in my high school play, "*I Remember
Mama*", by entering the pageant in the first place. I knew that
if I won Miss Teen London, I would have to give my lead role
to my understudy because the Miss Teen Canada pageant
dates would interfere with the last stages of rehearsal for the
school play. I loved acting and I was so excited to have this

lead role, but the potential for winning on a local, and then possibly (no matter how remote) national level, was too much for me to turn down.

My memory is a little hazy on the details of the night's events, so obviously I didn't have any memorable faux-pas that I had to deal with. The only painful sting was seeing James watch me from the audience. I wasn't good enough to be his, but he still took the time to see me compete.

Well, I, 'the Natural,' won against all the experienced models, and it was a glorious night. I had become Miss Teen London 1985 and I was headed to the Miss Teen Canada 1985 pageant. People swarmed to congratulate me; reporters pushed for pictures and interviews. It felt good to be appreciated for something – anything. With every new achievement, I would try to fill the insatiable void in my heart. The pain and emptiness would lighten for a time while I was being adorned and doted on, but the hole was never satisfied. The pain would once again intensify, and I would crave for another goal to accomplish in an endless attempt to squash the pain. As my life's bad choices replayed continually in my mind, I began to fight increasing thoughts of suicide as well. I worked relentlessly to appear like I had it all under control. I hid behind the smile on my face at all costs.

As I mentioned earlier, I knew that if I won Miss Teen London, I would have to give up my lead role. Oh, how I wished that Ms Bean would let me keep the role and try to do both the play and the pageant. But I knew it was unfair to put the whole school production at risk. If I won Miss Teen Canada then my life would be completely consumed with the title's commitments and ongoing events. I couldn't be that selfish, so my understudy took over for me. I have to admit that even though I managed to see the production, I felt very sad watching the play perform without me. I really wanted to 'eat my cake and have it too.'

Before I knew it, it was time for the Miss Teen Canada pageant week of rehearsals and tests on skills, talent and personality. Even though Strathroy was only less than two hours from Toronto, the pageant organizers planned for me to take the train to Toronto and pick me up in a limousine. I was nervous and excited to be taking the train by myself. I planned on using the time on the train to pump up my confidence with as much self pep talk as possible, but an interesting thing happened. At the time, I assumed it was a premonition, but later I realized the Holy Spirit was speaking to me. As I was running through all the possible senarios for the week, I could feel my appetite to win increase. And right in the middle of my own vision of winning, I heard a voice in my head say, "Julie, you will not win, but you will be in the top four finalists." What nonsense was this? I was going for the top prize like always. I would never settle ahead of time for a finalist position. Where did this voice come from? I spent the rest of the week at the pageant trying to ignore this message. No matter what, I was going to give it my all. I felt like I had nothing else going for me. I had to find value and worth somewhere because I certainly didn't feel it inside of me. Although I still prayed at night to God, He felt like a big cop in the sky. I was waiting for Him to punish me for all the bad things I had done. Surely He couldn't forgive me. I was damaged goods.

My fears about the girls disappeared quickly. Overall, they were very friendly. We were all strangers desperate to make new friends. Throughout the week, I tried to hide my strange eating habits. Every night we had large dinners and mealtime terrified me. I loved food, but I was scared to death of gaining a pound. I worried about every little pimple I might get too, even though I had been taking tetracycline for three years to help control my acne. And finding ways to discreetly pat down my oily face was not easy. During dance rehearsals, we had to wear running shoes, but my feet were only used to wearing dress shoes. (Remember, sweating was not for me at school.) The arches of my feet ached every day from not being used to the support in running shoes. When it came to the talent competition, I mentioned earlier that I had a monitor problem as I performed my solo. I had set my hopes on winning the talent portion of the pageant, but that was not to be. Yet, despite all my worries, concerns and mishaps, the week went along pretty well.

Finally the big night had arrived. It was time for the televised portion of the pageant. Butterflies were fluttering frantically in my stomach. And on top of it, the pageant organizers were scrambling to get everything and everyone ready because a snowstorm had hit the city. Several people were not able to make it to the studio. Even some of the makeup artists and hair stylists were unable to make it, so the few that did arrive, slapped the makeup on our faces and teased the life out of our hair in a factory line. I hated what they did to my hair. I looked like a punk rocker with my spikey hair instead of my usual soft curls. And for some reason, I was the only one who looked like they had a tan on their face. My makeup artist used a darker foundation, and then ignored my request to use taupe or purple eye shadow on my green eyes instead of light blue. I was not impressed. You can see for yourself on Youtube. Someone has posted the opening musical number and the medley musical number from the pageant.

After the opening musical number, we all ran backstage into one massive hall to change into our bright red, school-girl shirt and skirt outfits with our local winning sash. Then we raced into position at the stage entrance before the commercial break was done. It was organized chaos. I tried to catch my breath and calm my heart down before it was my turn to enter as Miss Teen London Julie vander Maden. My head was racing. I was exhilarated to be on television. I looked forward to giving my best performance. Yet at the same time, I couldn't help but think that James was probably watching with his new girlfriend. I thought about my family and friends who would be so shocked to hear of the date-rape that led to an internal hellish nine months for me. I thought about how the person I was in public was so different from the person I was in private. I recalled my thoughts of suicide. It was amazing. In that moment, waiting to go on stage, I was living the highest point of achievement in my life, and yet, it was the absolute, lowest point of my life personally, emotionally, and spiritually. I felt like I was being ripped in two. How could I be feeling such extreme emotions and yet, here I was struggling with just that.

"Breathe, just breathe," I tried to tell myself. "It's showtime."

I smiled, I walked, and I danced. Then it was time for the ten finalists to be chosen. My heart began to beat out of my chest again. A flood of relief came over me as I heard my name be called out as one of the ten. I had made it over the first hurdle.

Now it was time to speak. The ten finalists had to give a short, prepared answer about their goals in life. I don't remember all that I said, but I know it was about being a performer. It started something like, "To put a sparkle in someone's eye, or a smile on someone's face is what I hope to achieve with my goal." And I meant what I said. I loved being able to bring joy to people, even in such a frivolous way. I loved receiving the feedback after a performance, too. Performing was like creating something and giving birth to it. There was a sense of satisfaction in achieving something good after all the hard work. But even with all my sincerity, it was not enough. I had no idea of how it is possible to truly impact people's lives in this life and for eternity. In truth, nothing compares to sharing the love of Jesus and seeing that person's life change forever. A performance will always end, but the joy of salvation is everlasting.

Another commercial break. Then five finalists are chosen from the ten. Pounding, pounding. I can't slow my heart down. Then the words, "Our next finalist is Miss Teen London, Julie vander Maden." I can't believe it, but I'm so excited and relieved. I had made it over the second hurdle.

Now the five remaining finalists had to answer an impromptu question. This was the most challenging and nerve racking part of the pageant. I can't remember my question, but being someone who had to overcome stumbling over words earlier in my life, I was quite content with my response. My only little mistake was responding to the live audience instead of steadily responding to the camera. I was used to public speaking, so under this new stress, I did what was familiar. Speaking into a camera box was definitely *not* familiar to me.

I could almost taste the victory, except the words that had haunted me since the train ride kept playing back in my mind. "Julie, you are not going win, but you will be one of the four finalists." Really? Was this to be as far as I would go? No, it couldn't be. I had to win. What would I be going home to if I didn't? Yes, I would fulfill my Miss Teen London responsibilities, and I was honored to do so, but I was desperate for more. Hungry for more. Aching for more. I needed to achieve more. I was nothing if I didn't keep succeeding at something.

After the last commercial break, the five of us stood side by side for the final results. This was it. Was I going to beat that voice I heard on the train? The fourth runner-up was named. It wasn't me. I could feel my heart beating against my rib cage. The third runner-up was named. It wasn't me. I tried to remember to breathe. The second runner-up was called. It was still not me. Oh my goodness. It was down to me and Miss Teen Halifax-Dartmouth, Terry Smith. And the irony of it all was that she shared a joining room with me and my room-mate, Miss Teen Lethbridge, all week. She had made it clear to us that when it came down to it, she really, truly hoped that she *didn't* win because she didn't think she could handle the strenuous schedule and responsibilities. I, on the other hand, had expressed to her just how much I was willing to take on the position and just how much *I hoped to win*. And here we were standing together – the last two. We held hands and she repeatedly whispered, "I know you are going to win." All I could hear were the words in my head, "You are not going to win."

"And the first runner-up is.....Miss Teen London, Julie vander Maden." I was handed a huge bouquet of red roses and Miss Teen Halifax-Darmouth received the crown. I smiled, congratulated her, and wished with all my heart that the message I heard on the train was wrong!

MOMENTS OF REFLECTION:

Do you know when the Holy Spirit has tried to communicate with you?

How has it happened – an inner voice in your head, a dream, a vision, a person that you may or may not know spoke directly to you, a sermon message, an audible voice?

Have you ever wanted something so desperately that you gave 200% to try and attain it?

Was it worth all your effort in the end?

Do you pursue God with that same kind of fervency and desire?

Chapter Nine

BACK TO REALITY

"Good morning. I'm from the Strathroy's Age Dispatch newspaper. May I come in?"

I was still recovering from all the pageant hoopla, but I looked forward to doing interviews. My hair and makeup weren't as polished as I preferred, but at least I felt acceptable.

After the interview, it was time for some photos to be taken.

"I really like the mirror you have in the living-room. Do you mind if I try a shot of your reflection in the mirror?"

"Sure. Why not?" I liked to have a bit of an artistic flair in my style anyway.

When the paper came out, my mom was sure to buy several copies to keep for herself and to share with other family members.

Everyone liked the photo, but some, like me, noticed that it seemed a little distorted. Then I would tell them it was actually a reflection taken of me in the mirror. When I think of it, that photo provided a glimpse into the real me. In truth, I was distorted. On the outside, I looked pretty polished, but underneath the surface was a whole different Julie. A very broken person was trying to hide and disguise her agonizing pain.

Despite only placing 1st Runner-up to Miss Teen Canada 1985, I received quite a bit acclaim and praise locally. My small town, Strathroy, became a little more famous, and my boss, Joe Bernard, couldn't be happier for the publicity of his shoe store. Like I said earlier, if I couldn't sell many shoes, at least I was good for something.

I had several newspaper interviews and radio interviews. I received official letters from local politicians. I was even awarded the honor of Strathroy's Honorary Citizen and the key to the town by the mayor. It was only the fifth time to be awarded to someone, and I was the first female to receive it. Not bad for a girl who grew up with huge, foul smelling pigs running up and down the side house fence.

My family was proud of me and even my brother surprised me. The day I returned from Toronto, my brother left a yellow sticky note on the kitchen counter explaining how proud he was of me, and that he loved me. I can't tell you how much that meant after all our years of sibling fighting.

Life should have been great. And it was wonderful to have so many kind words spoken, and written about me. I was very honored, thankful and appreciative for such kindness, but when I would lie in bed at night, the darkness would awaken my inner torment. My heart would ache over James. Male attention was easy enough to find, but I wanted him. I was no longer anorexic, but bulimia had taken over with a vengeance. I loathed my bulimic binge/purge cycles. I was disgusted with myself; whereas, I felt in control when I was anorexic.

My weight began to fluctuate. My face became bloated. My thoughts would shift to Bruce and all the pain he had caused me. I still blamed myself for so much of it. I couldn't believe I would let myself get so low. I would agonize over my family and close friends ever finding out about what happened to me while I was trapped with Bruce. All I felt was shame, shame, *shame*. Then, I would end my nightly ritual torment with thoughts of how I could kill myself without pain. God seemed so far away. I didn't feel like I had the right to ask for His help. I *must* have disappointed Him beyond any chance of forgiveness. Hope was draining from me.

Nothingness

Written sometime in 1985

Windswept thoughts blow through my mind
Leaving me barren and without cause
Drifting with the misty clouds
Into unknown parts
I release my hold
The overpowering atmosphere
Swallows me up into oblivion
Where everything is useless, worthless, and without cause
Freedom evaporates, and slavery, too
Not one or the other is left to characterize my existence.

Julie vander Maden

My father had made such a big deal about me being too serious too early with boys, so now I took his advice to heart. I decided to just date – and date I did. I made my father eat his own words. We didn't have an answering machine, or voice-mail at that time, so my family often had to take messages from my many different suitors. The only problem was, at one point, I was dating around a dozen guys, and three had the same first name. My parents were afraid to ask for a last name because that would insinuate there was someone else. My father would become frustrated with me, so I would remind him that this was *his* doing.

I wish I could say that everyone I dated was a perfect gentleman, but when you think of yourself as dirt, you tend to attract dirt. Oh, I did manage to date some very nice guys, and I truly apologize to them for being such damaged goods. They deserved better. I had guys write music and poetry for me, sing for me, and basically wait hand and foot on me. I dated different nationalities and races. I dated guys that were conservative, preppy, rock musicians, brainiacs, rebels, backslidden Christians, actors, and suicidal ones. This one guy talked about suicide so much that he said we should commit suicide together. Another guy I met, while I was modeling swimsuits at a Boat Show, was a real gentleman and his looks reminded me of the actor Billy Crystal. We dated off and on, but I think I actually drove him away instead. Once I discovered that he had a strong Christian upbringing, I frequently bombarded him with questions about God until the wee hours of the morning. Ironically, he was struggling with his own faith at the time, so my incessant questioning must have tortured his backslidden heart.

To make matters worse, a girl that I grew up with in Sunday school, was killed in a head-on collision by a drunk driver. Although she was still only seventeen, she was engaged and was traveling to a hockey game with her fiancé, his cousin and his uncle. Kelly's fiancé was the only one who survived the crash–all because someone decided to drive drunk. Another young life was taken and I struggled to find the meaning in it all.

In any case, I was becoming more depressed and disgusted with myself. I didn't believe I deserved true love, so I threw all self-respect to the wind. Underage drinking was normal on my dates, and it took very little for me to be under the influence. When alcohol took over my mind, it wasn't difficult for guys to take over my body. This only increased my self-hatred and shame. I didn't know how much more worthless I could become. I was completely damaged goods.

LOST
Written April, 1983 during Workspare, 2 ½ years earlier.

Lost
Lost in a world of growing darkness
Lost in a place where our hands cannot meet
I'm lost
Lost in a maze with no way out.

Julie vander Maden

Psalm34:18 "The Lord is close to the broken-hearted and saves those who are crushed in spirit."

MOMENTS OF REFLECTION:

What is your opinion about dating? Personally, I believe it is pointless to date unless you are intent on marriage. Going out in mixed groups is fine, but too much alone time can lead to temptation. That's my opinion. What's yours? Have you thought it through?

We all know how to waste time on things and people that will not improve us. What have you wasted time on?

Do you have two different faces—one for public life and one for your private life? Are you aware of any mask that you might wear?

If you truly believe that God desires to use you to reach people, then does this belief change how you use your time?

Chapter Ten

TEENS STEP UP

Luke4:18 "The Spirit of the Lord is upon me, because he has anointed me to proclaim good news to the poor. He has sent me to proclaim freedom for the prisoners and recovery of sight for the blind, to set the oppressed free,"

Psalm147:3 "He heals the brokenhearted and binds up their wounds."

I know that I am dating myself when I say that I attended grade thirteen. It was the last year that Canada offered it, by the way. It was still a preparation year for those who intended on going to university. I had decided that taking Theater Arts as my major was too risky for getting decent, long-time employment. Instead, I planned to make English my major and Theater my minor when I went to university. With this in mind, a Creative Writing course that I wished to take was not offered at my high school, whereas Saunders high school in

London, Ontario did offer it. It took some persuading, but I was finally able to transfer to Saunders high school for my last year, despite residing in Strathroy.

Although I was so fragile emotionally, I attempted to make decisions for my future. As much as I wanted to get on with my life, leaving all the comforts of my small town where everyone loved me was not an easy thing to do. Attending Saunders meant walking into a new world of people who did not have a clue who I was. And I was *not* about to advertise that I was the reigning Miss Teen London, or 1st Runner-Up to Miss Teen Canada. I was terrified about how I would fit in. I was even more terrified about people possibly finding out about my deepest, ugly secrets. I had already dated a guy a year earlier who was well respected at Saunders high school. Dave was super sweet and smart. He wrote me several poems and he really wanted a deeper relationship. Dave was thinking long-term even though he was headed for university. But, of course, I refused to get closer, so I ended it. Who would want such damaged goods anyway? I can still see the hurt in his big, brown eyes. I am truly sorry for breaking his heart.

Adding to my concern was the fact that my doctor had decided it was time for me to take a break from the antibiotics I had been using long-term to treat my acne. Perfect timing. As September drew closer, my face exploded more and more. It reached an all-time record. I piled on the makeup in a desperate attempt to at least cover up the mess, but my face still looked like pizza. I used full, dramatic eye shadow and bright lipstick every single day, no matter what the occasion, in hopes of detracting people's attention away from the rest of my face.

Attending Saunders high school also meant that I needed to have some form of transportation. My dad managed to find a car that we could afford. I had to pay half for it, so my budget was extremely low. I have to say, though, that I loved my first car. It was a 1977, Buick Skyhawk, two-door hatchback, V6 engine, and more importantly, it was *red.* My acne may have been horrible to deal with, but at least I would arrive at my new school in a peppy, red car.

Ready or not, the time came for my first day of school in London. The day is a blur in my memory. Yet, I remember I got up extra early to put my artistic skills to the test as I applied spackles of makeup. I was traumatized by the acne mess on my face. I may have spent plenty of time preparing my physical mask, but for weeks I had already been preparing my invisible mask. I gave myself pep talks. I had to look like I had it altogether – strong, confident, carefree and likeable. No matter what, I could not afford to reveal even the slightest crack in my façade. People must not know the truth about me. Nobody wants to hang around damaged goods.

Looking back really is 20/20 vision. I had no idea that my desire to include a Creative Writing course into my last year of high school would become the catalyst for my dramatic turnaround. I have seen God use seemingly insignificant things to impact, guide or steer a person's direction in life many times since. When you look back, you may say to yourself, "If I had gone this way, this would have happened, if I had gone that way, that would have happened instead." Most of the time God uses ordinary things, ordinary people and ordinary situations to draw us closer to Him. Of course, we all know how common it is for a horrific event or loss to impact a person's decision to make huge, life changes. But if you really look closely at the person's life before the 'big interruption', you can see how God was already trying to get their attention in a more subtle way. They were just not paying attention. I see it in my own life. God sent those two, bold and courageous teenagers to teach me about Christ in my Sunday school class. In time, I let my emotions replace what I had been taught as truth. I doubted and gave into my misleading emotions. Every wrong choice I made was my own, not someone else's. No one put a gun to my head. I blew it. I compromised. I did not value myself as God valued me.

> Psalm139:14 says, "I praise you because I am fearfully and wonderfully made; your works are wonderful, I know that full well."

We will never know how valued we are until we change our lenses and look through God's eyes. God has never made junk and He never will. What we do with our own freewill is what can destroy us, or save us.

To my relief, it did not take long for me to make new friends at Saunders' District Collegiate. Of course, I was very guarded as to what I shared for the first while. I had already experienced how fame can affect people's attitudes towards a person while I was attending high school in Strathroy. After winning Miss Teen London and placing 1st Runner-Up to Miss Teen Canada, there were some people who had never given me the time of day before, but now became very interested in getting to know me. I have never been that kind of flaky person and a little fame was not going to change that. Even to this day, I have had the opportunity to meet several famous people, but I really do not care to just say 'hi'. I would much rather be given the opportunity to spend time with the person, so that they get to know me as well. Underneath a famous person's clothes, coiffed hair and makeup, is a human being that is struggling through life just like you and me. That's why Jesus shocked the religious people so much by choosing to hang out with the sick, poor and low life of society. If you search the scriptures, you will find that Jesus hung out with the sick, the blind, the paralyzed, lepers, tax collectors, prostitutes, adulterous women, children, Roman soldiers, beggars and even people of ethnic minorities, much to the religious leaders' disdain.

Mark2:16,17 says, "When the teachers of the law who were Pharisees saw him eating with the sinners and tax collectors, they asked his disciples: "Why does he eat with tax collectors and sinners?" On hearing this, Jesus said to them, "It is not the healthy who need a doctor, but the sick. I have not come to call the righteous, but sinners.""

I began to hang out with a couple of girls who were in a few of my classes. Terri was very sociable and bubbly while Diane was friendly and a little intense. Diane had naturally light blond hair and very blue eyes. She had an air of confidence about her without being snooty. When she would ask you a question, you felt like she was looking right through you. She was direct and to the point, but not mean. There was something different about her. It did not take long to find out through our conversations that she was a Christian, and one who was not afraid to let others know. Now when I say Christian. I do not mean someone who simply attends church. Many people call themselves Christian because they go to church at Christmas and Easter. That is not a Christian – that is someone who knows *of* Christ, but does not *know* Him in a personal relationship. I have met Prime Minister Pierre Elliot Trudeau, Robin Williams, Michael W. Smith and many other Christian recordings artists, but I have never had a relationship with any of them. Diane *knew* Christ like those two teenagers in my Sunday school class *knew* Christ. With my checkered past, I always felt God was the 'big cop in the sky' who had to be angry with me for all the bad decisions I had made. I felt He was distant and unapproachable. And the thought of forgiveness seemed like an impossibility. Not so to Diane. The way she spoke about Jesus was like someone speaking about her best friend. She spoke about how nothing can separate us from God's love and that He will never turn us away if we come humbly to Him.

Romans 8:15-17 says, "The Spirit you received does not make you slaves, so that you live in fear again; rather, the Spirit you received brought about **your adoption to sonship**. And by him we cry, **"Abba, Father."** The Spirit himself testifies with our spirit that **we are God's children**. Now if we are children, then we are heirs- **heirs of God and co-heirs with Christ**, if indeed we share in his sufferings in order that we may also share in his glory." (emphasis mine)

One of my favorite portions of scripture is Romans 8:31-39 which says, "What, then, shall we say in response to these things? **If God is for us, who can be against us?** He who did not spare his own Son, but gave him up for us all – how will he not also, along with him, graciously give us all things? Who will bring any charge against those whom God has chosen? It is God who justifies. Who then is the one who condemns? No one. Christ Jesus who died – more than that, who was raised to life – is at the right hand of God and is also interceding for us. **Who shall separate us from the love of Christ?** Shall trouble or hardship or persecution or famine or nakedness or danger or sword? As it is written: "For your sake we face death all day long; we are considered as sheep to be slaughtered." **No, in all these things we are more than conquerors through him who loved us.** For I am convinced that neither death nor life, neither angels nor demons, neither the present nor the future, nor any powers, neither height nor depth, **nor anything else in all creation, will be able to separate us from the love of God that is in Christ Jesus our Lord."** (emphasis mine)

Diane's invitation to come to her youth group was a pretty radical idea to me. The church I grew up in did not have a youth group. Once I was asked to put on a short skit with a handful of other teenagers for a special Sunday, but that was as close to having a youth group as we got. The idea of choosing to spend time at church besides Sunday morning was a totally foreign concept to me. Yet, I was attracted to what Diane had. I wanted a fresh start. I wanted to feel clean again inside. I did not want to be afraid to look up because I felt like God was frowning down at me. At least that was how I felt.

Diane invited me to other youth functions as well. Sometimes the youth group would go to roller-skating on Christian skate night which I had never heard of before. The only difference from other nights was what music was played. I did not recognize any of the Christian artists, but I liked the music. I was surprised to hear this modern form of Christian music because all I knew were hymns played on the church organ by our little, old lady organist.

I found acceptance from Diane and her brothers, Cody and Redman. I started to make friends at the youth group when I attended their Bible studies and different events. I saw teen-agers stand up for what they believed in without any excuse or embarrassment. This was the meaning of life to them and not just a boring Sunday morning ritual. It was refreshing. Of course, the youth pastor and leaders were nice, but it was the bold-ness and acceptance of individual youth that impacted my life.

MOMENTS OF REFLECTION:

Do you call yourself a Christian?

When did you decide to follow Christ?

How real is faith to you in your everyday life? Do you include Jesus in all aspects of your life, or just on Sunday mornings?

Do you feel a responsibility to reach out to your friends or those close around you?

Do you feel too young and inexperienced to be used by God to reach those around you?

Do you have a heart's desire to be used by God, but something is holding you back? Is it fear, or insecurities?

Do you feel unprepared to speak to people?

Do you try to downplay your faith around non-Christians?

Have you prayed and asked God to help give you the words to say in situations where you feel incompetent?

Have you spent time memorizing scriptures that have helped you, so you, in turn can readily share them with others at the appropriate time?

Chapter Eleven

COMING HOME

B y the end of September, I was a changed person. No lightning strikes, no fireworks, no eureka moment happened to me. I did not have one particular moment where I walked to a church altar, or experienced a miraculous conversion like some people do. Since I had already been introduced to Jesus by those two brave teenagers in Sunday school years earlier, I found my experience to be more of a coming home, like the story of the prodigal son. I began to look at God differently. I started to understand His unconditional love. I learned how God chooses to forgive us as we surrender our lives wholly to Him. I asked for God's forgiveness for all the things I had done, and for straying from him. Amazingly, this time I truly felt his forgiveness. I had believed in wrong thinking of who God is and what His character is like. He is not the 'big cop in the sky' who is eagerly waiting for me to mess up, so He can hammer me with his judgment. That's why He sent Jesus to come and die on the cross for our sins (our faults, imperfections, shortcomings, lies, deceit, etc) instead, so that we do not have to *pay* the price for ourselves. Only perfection in the form of Jesus, God's own Son, could actually heal and restore our relationship to a holy, righteous God who cannot, by His pure existence, be in the presence of sin. I now understood that personally.

Words like 'sin', 'transgression', and 'iniquity' are basically all the same. A little 'white' lie is just as much a sin as murdering someone; only the consequences are different. Both separate us from our Creator and leave us desperately seeking for peace in all the wrong places and in all the wrong things. No amount of fame, wealth, or power can ever fill the emptiness each human being has inside of them. No matter how much we try to find self-esteem, significance and security on our own, there is always a deep ache of emptiness left inside of us. We were created to have an eternal relationship with a God who is more powerful and amazing than our finite minds can imagine. When we finally realize that this life is only the training ground for life in eternity, it opens up our minds to true purpose, true significance and true self-esteem. When we understand that we are loved unconditionally for 'who we are' and not 'what we can do' in this world, it changes everything. And that's what I experienced.

Giving the control of your life over to Jesus does not mean you will never have any problems, pain, or suffering. What it does mean is that you will always have a loving God who will help you walk through any trial of life with a deep sense of inner peace. You may be 'freaking' on the outside some times, but if Jesus is on the throne of your life, He will give you 'a peace that passes all understanding' (Phillipians4:7)

Psalm 103:8,10-12 says, "The Lord is compassionate and gracious, slow to anger, **abounding in love**....he does not treat us as our sins deserve or repay us according to our iniquities. **For as high as the heavens are above the earth, so great is his love for those who fear him; as far as the east is from the west, so far has he removed our transgressions from us.**" (emphasis mine)

I found myself praying to God throughout the day. " What is prayer and how do you do it?" you might be saying. Simply put, it's talking to God out loud or in your mind. It's having a conversation. That means you also wait for God to respond, whether it is through a still, small voice in your head, or a scripture or vision that is brought to your mind, or a revelation through someone's teaching. God speaks to us in many ways, but we have to have a heart that is open to listen.

I also bought myself a new Bible that was easier to understand, and I scribbled and highlighted the life out of it. Today you can buy many versions of the Bible, so it is important to find one that you easily understand. And do not be afraid to write in it. Of course, you can find the Bible in every form of today's technology, too. Whatever helps to bring God's word to life in your heart is most important. I found that scripture started to make sense to me for the first time. But most importantly, I felt clean again. I was no longer afraid of God. I now wanted to run to Him. I started relinquishing my control for the first time. I put Christ on the throne of my life instead of myself, and the ache in my soul finally ceased.

2Corinthians 5:17-19 says, "Therefore, if anyone is in Christ, the new creation has come: **The old has gone, the new is**

here! All is from God, who reconciled us to himself through Christ and gave us the ministry of reconciliation: that God was reconciling the world to himself in Christ, **not counting people's sins against them**. And he has committed to us the message of reconciliation." (emphasis mine)

An interesting thing did happen to me after I placed Christ on the throne of my heart. The desire to binge and purge food, as well as any desire to starve myself, *completely* left me. I couldn't believe it. Once the hole in my life was finally filled with the only One that could ever bring complete peace – Jesus – my impulse to control my weight at any destructive cost was eliminated. My years of battling anorexia and bulimia came to a screeching halt once and for all. It was amazing.

I wish I could say that because I no longer had a problem with food that I did not have to think about my weight anymore either. But unfortunately, I had ruined my metabolism so badly that it took at least a couple years for my body to achieve a normal metabolic rate again. Years of starving myself and confusing my body about when and how much I would eat, had put my body into 'starvation mode'. I had trained my body to be prepared for times of fasting, so any food I now ate was saved as fat. This is a natural response for the body and it can happen to anyone who tries to recover from an eating disorder. Obviously, this makes the recovery more challenging, as the last thing someone concerned with her weight wants–is fast gaining weight! If she is not truly determined to work through the process of normalizing her metabolism, the temptation to return to the eating disorder can be overpowering. This is what made God's intervention in this area of my life so wonderful. I was so thankful that He had taken away any desire to return to my eating disorders. It was truly a miracle.

MOMENTS OF REFLECTION:

Have you ever read the story about the 'Prodigal Son"? If not, I encourage to do so in Luke15:11-32

Have you ever stopped to think that sin, of any kind, is the same in God's eyes? It's not harder for Him to forgive you of one type of a sin over another. The consequence of sin is a different story though. There are definitely harder consequences for murdering someone than for telling a white lie.

'As far as the east is from the west' creates a line of infinity. That's how far God throws our sins away when He forgives us. Have you accepted that God chooses to forgive your sins like that, or do you remind God over and over again about what you have done in the past?

Do you forgive like God when people sin against you? Or do you try to forgive them only to pick it up again and throw it back in their faces?

Are you talking to God every day?

Are you taking the time to be quiet and wait for God to talk to you?

Are you spending time reading the Bible? Do you highlight and memorize scriptures that stand out to you, or do you read a quick verse and rush out for the day?

Who's on the throne of your heart–you, God, or something else?

Chapter Twelve

TRAGEDY STRIKES

I have always appreciated someone who 'tells it straight'. You know the kind of person – someone who presents both the pros and the cons in a balanced way. Well, I hope to be that kind of person. It irks me when well-meaning people suggest coming to Jesus means a free ticket to a problem-free life. Nothing could be further from the truth. Just because you accept Jesus as your Lord and Savior does not mean that you will never have a problem again in your life. Yes, Christ will give you peace and the strength to endure all things. We are to give Christ our burdens and he will help us. Many times we will see miracles happen throughout our lives, *but* we will still have those times when we wonder why God didn't intervene. That's when we have to remember that our hope does not lie in this world. Our lives here are but a vapor, but we will live in heaven for eternal. This world is our training ground – and sometimes training hurts. You may find that standing up for Christ could cost you a friendship, or even a job. In several parts of the world, standing up for Christ could cost you your very life, even to this day. Sometimes doing the right thing could cost you more money, or make life more inconvenient. Because we live in a fallen world, we still experience the effects of living here. There will still be times of sickness and chances of accidents, and a laundry list of other stuff that isn't pleasant to endure.

There are two major points I want to make here. First, accepting Jesus as your Lord and Savior means you become a new creation in Christ. You become righteous before God because God is now looking at you through Jesus. Since He is perfect, holy and without sin, Jesus became the perfect sacrifice for all mankind. We are now welcome into God's presence because of Jesus. But God does not want to leave us simply forgiven. The rest of our time here on earth is spent renewing our minds and becoming more like Christ. That is basically what sanctification means. God always accepts us where we are, but he doesn't leave us there. He wants us to grow in wisdom and knowledge and to develop spiritual gifts. He encourages us to take control of our minds and actions. You have probably heard of the saying that if something isn't growing, it's dying. It's true for our Christian walk. If we are comfortable with just saying the words "I accepted Christ" without putting any effort into becoming more like Christ in *every* area of our lives, then most likely the decision was not sincere. Christ will change the lives of those who *want* to be changed and other people *will* begin to see the fruit.

Second, if we are truly desiring to follow Christ with all our heart, mind and soul, then we will eventually yearn to share God's message of love and salvation with the rest of the world, in whatever way God leads us. I am not saying that we will all want to become missionaries. I know this has not happened to me. Or that we will all feel impressed to write a book. What I am saying is that wherever you are planted, you will develop a desire to impact the lives of those around you. You will grow where you are planted, and you will let your light shine.

I don't want you to take my word for all of this, so here are some scriptures that will help.

Philippians 4:7 "And the peace of God, which transcends all understanding, will guard your hearts and your minds in Christ Jesus."

Philippians 4:13 "I can do all this through him who gives me strength."

James 4:14b-15,17 "What is your life? You are a mist that appears for a little while and then vanishes. Instead, you ought to say, 'If it is the Lord's will, we will live and do this or that.'.... If anyone, then, knows the good they ought to do and doesn't do it, it is sin for them."

Romans 12:2 "Do not conform to the pattern of this world, but be transformed by the renewing of your mind. Then you will be able to test and approve what God's will is – his good, pleasing and perfect will."

John15:20 "Remember what I told you: 'A servant is not greater than his master.' If they persecuted me, they will persecute you also. If they obeyed my teaching, they will obey yours also."

Christ promises to walk with us through the trials of life, and sometimes He even carries us. When we turn to Jesus, we never again have to go through something alone. Even if the world has abandoned us, Christ never will.

Deuteronomy 31:8 "The Lord himself goes before you and will be with you; he will never leave you nor forsake you. Do not be afraid; do not be discouraged."

Little did I know that I was about to face more pain despite having placed Christ back on the throne of my life. Diane and I had become good friends, and I was becoming even better friends with her younger brother, Cody. It wasn't long before we started becoming more than just friends. I was so thrilled to have Christ in my life and now I had a guy who shared the same passion. It felt like it was too much to ask for. The day we started dating should have been nothing but new excitement and joy, but instead I found myself in total shock.

It was Sunday, October 7th, 1985. My parents had planned to go to mom's twin sister's place in the country. My aunt and uncle had three kids, fraternal twin boys, and a younger daughter. For some reason my parents cancelled. I think they were unsure of the weather. Later that day we received a call from my aunt. That afternoon my twin cousins decided to ride their four-trax bike on the back roads. The weather was completely grey. Stephen, the blond straight-haired twin, was sitting behind Stuart, the curly brunette twin. In order to return to their home, Stuart had to cross a country highway. He quickly looked both ways and started to cross the highway. The last words he heard from his brother were "Stuart *no!*" On that very grey day, on a grey highway was a grey van that Stuart did not notice when he quickly looked both ways. The van was traveling too fast to avoid them. My cousins were hit straight on. Stuart and Stephen went flying through the air. Stephen flew the furthest. My aunt said Stuart was badly beat up, but would eventually be fine. Stephen was on life support with severe brain trauma and several other major injuries. The next day he was gone. He was only sixteen. What made this even more eerie was the fact that my family was supposed to be there for the afternoon. Norm, my younger brother, who was almost sixteen, would normally be the one riding with Stuart on the bike. It could have just as easily been my own brother.

It is hard to relay the intensity of emotions that I experienced, but I can tell you without any doubt that my restored faith in Christ carried me through that time. I can't begin to imagine how I would have handled it just a couple months earlier.

Over the years, I have seen people with miraculous doctor-confirmed healings; I have seen money arrive just in the knick of time; I have seen job opportunities arise in perfect circumstances, and I have seen people come to know Christ after years of praying. Despite all these amazing miracles, I have also seen people die instead of receive healing, and I have seen people suffer unjustly. To this day, I do not have all the answers as to why some people receive healing and others do not, or why some people seem to go through so much suffering while others live relatively free of pain.

1Cor.13:12 "For now we see only a reflection as in a mirror; then we shall see face to face. Now I know in part; then I shall know fully, even as I am fully known."

Like this scripture says, 'we know in part'. Right now we can't always see the 'big picture'. It can be frustrating and baffling, but one day in heaven we will understand why God allowed certain things to happen. We have to trust that God is good *all* the time even when we don't understand what is going on. Despite the freshness of my faith, I decided to trust that God has a reason for everything even when I don't see it at the time. I clung to His goodness and ran to Him for comfort in my grief.

2Corinthians 1:3,4 "Praise be to the God and Father of our Lord Jesus Christ, the Father of compassion and the God of all comfort, who comforts us in all our troubles, so that we can comfort those in any trouble with the comfort we ourselves receive from God."

Despite working through the several stages of grief, my faith continued to grow. And I saw my parents and brother develop their own personal faith in the Lord, too. Going to church was no longer a 'Sunday morning ritual', but something that my whole family looked forward to doing. Everyone was reading their Bibles and seeking God in a new and fresh way.

Colossians 2:6 "So then, just as you received Christ Jesus as Lord, continue to live your lives in him, rooted and built up in him, strengthened in the faith as you were taught, and over-flowing with thankfulness."

Life continued on, and before I knew it, my reign was coming to an end as Miss Teen London. In February, 1986, I passed on my Miss Teen London crown to the next reigning contestant. Cody and Diane's mother sewed me a dress just for the event. It was so wonderful to see how far I had come in a year since both the Miss Teen London and Miss Teen Canada pageants. I was no longer the same girl dealing with eating disorders, heartbreak, and suicidal thoughts. Christ had made me a new creation. I had finally discovered an inner peace that only Jesus can give.

Another huge step of recovery for me was to build up enough courage to share with Cody about my date-rape relationship and my promiscuity that followed as a result. I have to admit that I was scared he might reject me even though I knew Jesus had forgiven me once and for all. I didn't know if Cody could handle my colored past, but if we were to continue to grow in our relationship, I had to be honest about everything. No more secrets in the closet. No matter how uncomfortable it was for me.

YOU FORGAVE MY HORRIBLE PAST

Written February 10th, 1986 for Cody after I shared about the date rape with Bruce and my demise with other guys thereafter.

Hanging over my head was a piece of my horrible past,
And unrelenting untold truth,
With each day it grew darker and hung heavier over my head.
I never knew if I could be freed.
Finally, when the weight became too much,
I destroyed this stealthy cloud by mounting unknown courage.
With utmost terror, I expelled the truth,
While waiting for my expected fate.
To my delighted surprise my doom did not come.
You did not shun me or reject me.
Overwhelming joy poured into my heart and filled my soul with life.
Your understanding and forgiveness were like the sweetest sounds of music to my ears.

My love for you bounded higher and higher.
And I could have hugged you until your body broke.
How special you are to me
And what meaning you bring to my life.
Never again will a piece of my horrible past hang
over my head.
Not as long as you are here with me.

Julie vander Maden

Back at school, I heard that Saunders' theater arts department was to put on a Variety Show of various skits and musical numbers that April. Of course, I had to be a part of it. I had so much fun doing what I loved without all the baggage I used to carry. I sang "I Hate Men". Then I had the opportunity to play a marionette puppet in another skit. The icing on the cake was my unforgettable curtain call. The last skit ended in a huge whip cream pie fight. Clearly no one thought that it might be a good idea to clean the stage, at least a little, before doing the curtain call. My last costume was a white, flouncy skort with fluffy, pink bunny ears. As I entered from the side curtain to the middle upstage, and then turned to begin walking downstage towards the audience, I slipped on a pile of whip cream. My feet went flying up into the air while I landed with a thud on my back. The momentum carried me all the way up to the front of the stage, until the slide of whip cream stopped and I was thrown back into a seated position. No one could have planned it better! It looked like I had done it on purpose, for sure. Can you picture me with my white skort pulled up, while my backside and legs made their way to the front of the stage 'spread eagle'? Then imagine my legs slamming down onto the stage and my body springing into a seated position with pink bunny ears bouncing on my head. Oh, how I wish someone had videotaped it. I probably could have made some money on 'America's Funniest Videos' or on some other similar show The audience was roaring with laughter, so like a true performer, I went with it. I smiled, shrugged my shoulders with my hands out to my sides, as if to say, "What are you going to do?"

Ecclesiastes 3:1,4 "There is a time for everything, and a season for every activity under the heavens:...a time to weep and a time to **laugh**, a time to mourn and a time to dance," (emphasis mine)

I may have been going through a season of mourning, but this was definitely a great chance to laugh. God's word speaks about the benefit of laughter.

Proverb 17:22 "A cheerful heart is good medicine, but a crushed spirit dries up the bones."

MOMENTS OF REFLECTION:

Have you ever lost someone close to you?

How did you handle it?

God performs miracles all the time, but when you don't receive a particular miracle, do you get angry at God? Do you question His intentions, or do you accept His will despite your loss?

It's important to remember the goodness of God never changes, even when we are in the midst of trials. At those times it may be very difficult to understand, but it doesn't change the truth that 'God is good all the time; all the time God is good'. During times of trials, do your run to God first, or do you seek everywhere else for comfort and guidance? Psalm18:2 says, "The Lord is my rock, my fortress and my deliverer; my God is my rock, in whom I take refuge, my shield and the horn of my salvation, my stronghold."

Do you have someone in your life that you feel has the spiritual wisdom to give you guidance when you are struggling?

Chapter Thirteen

THE SPIRITUAL BATTLES CONTINUES

1 Peter 5:7-10 "Cast all your anxiety on him because he cares for you. Be alert and of sober mind. **Your enemy the devil prowls around like a roaring lion looking for someone to devour.** Resist him, standing firm in the faith, because you know that the family of believers throughout the world is undergoing the same kind of sufferings. And the God of all grace, who called you to his eternal glory in Christ, after you have suffered a little while, will himself restore you and make you strong, firm and steadfast." (emphasis mine)

The Holy Spirit works diligently to guide us into a deeper relationship with Christ if we take the time to listen to his voice. At the same time, Satan (aka the devil, Lucifer, Prince of the power of the air, antichrist, Beelzebub, etc) does everything in his power to pull us away from Christ. One of his favorite things to use is our past. He loves to bring up old sins and painful situations to rub in our faces, so that we will focus on our past failures and pain instead of our new life in Christ as forgiven children of our Abba Father. Satan also looks for areas in our life that still need to be dealt with in order to live stronger and freer in Christ. Remember, I said that God accepts us where we are at when we come to Him, but He never leaves us there. This is part of our sanctification (the setting apart of believers and the process of becoming more Christ-like). We spend are whole life removing unwanted baggage and traits and slowly replace them with the mind of Christ. As we learn more about God's word, we discover what is righteous and what is not. God is patient and kind, so He does not throw the Bible at us and expect us to be perfect in an instant. He reveals things to us as we are ready to deal with them.

Well, it soon became time for me to deal with a particular area of my life. You see, I already had demonic experiences as a child. Then in my younger teens I thought I had received a visit from a past relative. I had always been very interested in psychics and astrology growing up. I used to read daily horoscopes and I even visited a psychic once at age sixteen. During my junior high days, one of my girlfriends had an Ouija board that we used to play. We all thought it was innocent. I had no idea of the door I was opening.

When I was a very young child, sometimes at night I would see a shadow of a man standing beside my bed. The moonlight would shine through my window and I could see the silhouette of a man wearing a long trench coat and a fedora hat. He would just stand there looking at me. Terrified, I would put my face under the covers even though it was hard to breathe. One time when I put my face under the covers, it felt like the weight of the man fell across my legs. I laid there paralyzed in fear for what seemed like hours until it finally lifted. I was *not* dreaming and he appeared several times. If you believe in God, you have to believe in Satan. Satan will do anything to keep us from giving our lives to Christ. Children have fresh minds that are ready to absorb everything around them. Satan will do anything to capture those young minds.

At fourteen, I stayed home a day from school sick with a cold. I was in the living room when I heard the shuffle of footsteps. No one else was home, but our family dog, Missy, and she was in the living room with me. Chills ran down my spine as I listened. I couldn't believe my ears. The walk was so familiar. I could have sworn that it was my deceased grandfather walking in the kitchen. He had had a very distinct shuffling walk because of his stroke when I was two years old. Of course, I eventually got my nerve up and I ventured out to the kitchen. Nothing was there.

Another incident occurred while I was getting ready for high school. Missy, my Shetland sheepdog, was sitting in the bathroom while I was doing my hair and makeup. Suddenly she bolted out of the bathroom and ran into the dining room. I hadn't heard a sound. Everyone else had left the house already, so I, once again, was the only one home. I came out of the bathroom to see what was wrong. Missy was looking up into the corner of the dining-room, as if she was looking directly into someone's face, and barking madly for about 30 seconds. Her hair stood up on end. Again, I felt a strong presence. I was so freaked out that I called my mom at work to tell her about it.

I also had a time while I was doing homework at the dining room table at night. The window across the table from me had the curtains still open, so all I saw was the blackness of the night. While I was working on my homework, I began to sense someone was watching me. When I finally glanced up, I saw what looked like the face of a demon in the window. I didn't tell anyone about it. Needless to say, I got up and closed the curtains quickly after that.

And lastly, I used to have demonic dreams that terrified me. The spirit world was very real to me in my dreams.

I want you to understand that I am not sharing all of this to promote Satan, or to create fear in you. These were very real experiences for me that I did not know how to handle. I did not know what to do. I did not know that I *could* do anything.

Now that I was living for Christ, I assumed all this weird stuff, especially the demonic dreams, would all cease. But it did not. As the year worn on, I was experiencing an increasing number of demonic dreams and by June, 1986, horrifying day-time visions started even while I was at a Christian camp. There were several times when I was driving home from London that I felt an overwhelming urge to drive off of the road and it was all I could do to stop myself. I knew it wasn't me because I was loving life now. I just did not understand why this was happening to me. I would pray for protection, but it would happen again.

The most disturbing incidents happened at Cody and Diane's house. Because I lived in Strathroy, but attended high school and, now, church youth group in London, there were many nights that their parents allowed me to stay over. They lived in a beautiful two- story house with a grand staircase in the front foyer. It was here, that I repeatedly saw the shadow of a man standing upstairs by the middle, foyer window.

It wasn't until this last incident occurred that I finally told Cody and Diane's parents about what was happening. One Saturday night I stayed over in their guest room. It was located in the basement beside a large rec room. The next morning everyone went off to church, but I stayed behind so that I could work on my photography project. I hadn't had time to take pictures earlier and I was hoping for great outdoor winter photos. There was a fresh blanket of snow outside, so I knew I could get some good art shots for my project.

I had devotions in bed, showered, and then I went upstairs to the kitchen to get some breakfast before heading outside. Earlier I assumed that everyone went to church, but then I thought I had to be wrong. After staying over night at their house so many times, I had become accustomed to all the house noises and the movements of everyone upstairs. I heard the sound of walking around, the shower running and the blow-dryer. So, I assumed Diane must have stayed home, like me. I figured she would be down when I finished taking photos outside. Well, you can imagine the shock on my face when everyone returned from church and the first person that walked in the door was – Diane.

Everyone could see that I was telling the truth, so I also shared about my sightings of the man upstairs by the foyer window. Being a Christian family, they decided it was important to pray and see if there was anything unholy that may have been brought into the house. They prayed for forgiveness of any unknown sins. Then they dedicated the house to the Lord again, and commanded anything that was not of God to go in Jesus' name. In this way, whatever was not of God – had to go.

They also suggested that I make an appointment to see our church pastor. Clearly I had to do something about these experiences and fear was not the way to deal with it. That much I knew for sure.

This visit was a turning point for me. I learned that I had to ask specifically for forgiveness for my dabbling in astrology, fortune-telling and the Ouija board. These are all mild forms of the occult. Satan had been using this as a door into my mind to fill me with fear. Although he could no longer possess me as a Christian, he could certainly harass me. As long as I allowed fear to rule my mind, then I was powerless. I had to learn who I was in Christ and shut this door once and for all.

1John4:1-4 "Dear friends, do not believe every spirit, but **test the spirits to see whether they are from God**, because many false prophets have gone out into the world. This is how you can recognize the Spirit of God: Every spirit that acknowledges that Jesus Christ has come in the flesh is from God, but every spirit that does not acknowledge Jesus is not from God. This is the spirit of the **antichrist**, which you have heard is coming and even now is already in the world. You, dear children, are from God and have overcome them, because **the one who is in you is greater than the one who is in the world.**" (emphasis mine)

Who is in us? Jesus lives in us when we surrender the control of our lives over to Him. Who is in this world? Satan. And he is like a roaring lion seeking whom he can devour. We must know who we are in Christ. If we daily confess our sins, ask for forgiveness and continually seek after God's own heart, then we can walk with confidence in God's power because 'greater is He (Christ) who is within us than he (Satan) who is within the world'.

1Corinthians 12:8-10 "To one there is given through the Spirit the message of wisdom, to another the message of knowledge by means of the same Spirit, to another faith by the same Spirit, to another gifts of healing by that one Spirit, to another miraculous powers, to another prophecy, **to another distinguishing between spirits**, to another speaking in different kinds of tongues, and to still another the interpretation of tongues. **All these are the work of one and the same Spirit, and he gives them to each one, just as he determines.**" (emphasis mine)

I learned that once I closed the door to my past involvement in mild forms of the occult, Satan no longer had the right to harass me. I also learned that God gives people different gifts to help the body of Christ. One of these gifts is the ability to discern between godly and ungodly spirits. Once I understood that there was nothing to fear because Christ is Lord of my life, I could finally allow the Holy Spirit to guide me and teach me on how to use this spiritual gift.

Mark 16:17-18 NIV "And these signs will accompany those who believe: **In my name they will drive out demons**; they will speak in new tongues; they will pick up snakes with their hands; and when they drink deadly poison, it will not hurt them at all; they will place their hands on sick people, and they will get well." (emphasis mine)

145

Satan has *no* power over us, only what *we let him have* by not keeping our hearts pure and allowing fear to take control.

1John 4:18 "There is no fear in love. Because perfect love drives out fear, because fear has to do with punishment. The one who fears is not made perfect in love."

2Timothy 1:7 "For the Spirit God gave us does not make us timid (or fearful), but gives us power, love and self-discipline (or a sound mind)." (added parentheses mine)

2Timothy 1:7 became my favorite scripture. From that time forward I knew that if I ever had a demonic dream, or sensed an evil presence, I could quote this scripture. I reminded myself that God gives me *power, love* and a *sound mind*, so that I can command any evil spirit to leave in Jesus' name.

My second favorite scripture I loved to quote out loud, so that whatever principality around could hear me say, "Greater is he who is within me than he who is in the world."(1John4:4) In this way, I was standing my ground on God's word and I was reaffirming my position in God's family.

I also knew that I had to take control of my thought life because if I let my thoughts wander, Satan could easily influence my thinking. I did not want daytime demonic visions to gain more control, that's for sure.

2Corinthians 10:3-5 "For though we live in the world, we do not wage war as the world does. The weapons we fight with are not the weapons of the world. On the contrary, they have divine power to demolish strongholds. We demolish arguments and every pretension that sets itself up against the knowledge of God, **and we take captive every thought to make it obedient to Christ.**" (emphasis mine)

Now you might be thinking, "How do I take every thought captive to make it obedient to Christ?" First of all, we cannot stop a thought from popping into our heads, but we can choose whether or not to dwell on that new thought. This is where we have to exercise our freewill. Do we choose to think on a demonic thought, lustful thought, greedy thought, hateful thought, jealous thought, depressing thought – you get the picture – or do we mentally tells ourselves '*stop.*' If we give into the thought and choose to dwell on it, then we open ourselves up to fear, greediness, jealousy, lust, depression, etc. But, if we choose to mentally shout '*stop*' and command the thought to go in the name of Jesus, we are successfully taking control of our thoughts and bringing them into Christ's obedience. And by choosing to think on something else, say, a scripture, a worship song, a sermon, or any other good thought, we are actively working to keep that wrong thinking out of our heads. Sometimes that might mean you have to repeatedly, several times a day, take control of an ungodly thought and replace it with a godly one, but that's why it's called spiritual warfare. Satan doesn't give up without a fight and we have to keep reminding ourselves–and him–just who is in charge of our life – Jesus.

Ephesians 6:10-18 "Finally, be strong in the Lord and in his mighty power. Put on the full armor of God, so that you can take your **stand** against the devil's schemes. For our struggle is not against flesh and blood, but against the rulers, against the authorities, against the powers of this dark world and against the spiritual forces of evil in the heavenly realms. Therefore put on the full armor of God, so that when the day of evil comes, you may be able to **stand** your ground, and after you have done everything, to **stand. Stand** firm then, with the belt of truth buckled around your waist, with the breastplate of righteousness in place, and with your feet fitted with the readiness that comes from the gospel of peace. In addition to all this, take up the shield of faith, with which you can extinguish all the flaming arrows of the evil one. Take the helmet of salvation and the sword of the Spirit, which is the word of God. And pray in the Spirit on all occasions with all kind of prayers and requests. With this in mind, be alert and always keep on praying for all the Lord's people." (emphasis mine)

I think it's pretty obvious that God wants us to *stand* firm; *stand* our ground on his word. Four times the word 'stand' is mentioned in this passage. Then, once we have learned that we must 'stand', God goes on to show us *how* to stand in the following verses. As my pastor in Florida has said, "As Christians, we do not fight for victory; we fight *from* victory."

First, is the Belt of Truth. In biblical times, this area on our body was referred to as the 'seat of our emotions'. Therefore, it makes perfect sense that God wants us to protect our emotions with his truth. As well, one of Satan's names is the 'Father of Lies', so it is obvious that we, as Christians, need to focus on the truth in order to destroy his lies.

Second, is the Breastplate of Righteousness. This is not accomplished by our own works. We are not righteous, in and of ourselves, but rather, as we accept Jesus' work done on the cross, we put on his righteousness in faith. The day we put our faith in Christ, we became righteous, just like we did not sin. Jesus *lived* and *died* for us. Jesus lived for us by obeying

The Spiritual Battles Continues

all the commandments that we couldn't; therefore, his perfect life record allows us *positional* righteousness when we ask for forgiveness of our sins and place Jesus on the throne of our lives. From this point on, we achieve *practical* righteousness throughout our lives as we allow the Holy Spirit to conform us more and more like Jesus. We must always remember that our righteousness *before* accepting Christ is filthy rags (Isaiah 64:6), but *after* accepting Christ, we are clothed in his righteousness.

Third, is the Gospel of Peace fitted on our feet (the Shoes of Peace). If you think about it, when we are willing to share God's message of love and salvation to the world, we are walking into the enemy's territory. Satan does not want anyone to be freed from bondage, so our feet need to be ready to advance, fully aware of any obstacles that Satan may put in our way. Even in biblical times, Roman soldiers wore specific sandals (called Caligae) for battle. These particular sandals had nail cleats on the bottom (called hobnailed soles), so that it made it easier for the Roman soldier to stand firm in the sand or dirt while fighting. Likewise, the shoes of peace stabilize us in the battles of life.

Philippians 4:6,7 "Do not be anxious about anything, but in every situation, by prayer and petition, with thanksgiving, present your requests to God. And the peace of God, which transcends all understanding, will guard your hearts and your minds in Christ Jesus."

Fourth, is the Shield of Faith. Roman soldiers carried shields made of three sheets of wood glued together and covered in leather in order to stop flaming arrows from burning through. They also increased their protection by linking together with other soldiers to create a barrier formation around, and above, themselves. Likewise, the more we hear the word of God, the more our faith increases. Secondly, as we link together with other believers in Christ, we are able to build up each other's faith with encouraging words, emotional support and meeting physical needs. Hence, the more we put our faith in Christ and in his word, the more our shield of faith will squash all Satan's doubts concerning God's power and authority. This is how we 'quench all the fiery darts of the wicked'.

Fifth, is the Helmet of Salvation. When we receive Christ, we put on the helmet of salvation. This helmet protects our minds from doubting the truth of God's eternal purpose for us. With our minds protected, we are able to discern between spiritual truth and spiritual deception. The helmet of salvation destroys all doubts about our salvation, so Satan cannot weaken us.

John 10:7-10 ""Therefore Jesus said again, "Very truly I tell you, I am the gate for the sheep. All who have come before me are thieves and robbers, but the sheep have not listened to them. I am the gate; whoever enters through me will be saved. They will come in and go out, and find pasture. The thief comes only to steal and kill and destroy; I have come that they may have life, and have it to the full.""

Sixth, is the Sword of the Spirit. The Word of God, the bible, is our strongest offensive and defensive weapon against Satan's attacks. In the desert, even Jesus used the Word of God against Satan's temptations. The more we actively hide the Word of God in our hearts by reading and memorizing it regularly, the stronger our sword of the Spirit will be.

1John 2:14 "I write to you, dear children, because you know the father. I write to you, fathers, because you know him who is from the beginning. I write to you, young men, because you are strong, and the word of God lives in you, and you have overcome the evil one."

Lastly, after we symbolically put on the full armor of God, we are to pray in the Spirit, praying according to God's heart and priorities, so that we draw spiritual strength. We are powerless without complete reliance on God in all things. Prayer keeps our focus on Christ and off of ourselves. These are the tools that God has given us, so that we may be able to truly – stand. Just because you have given your life to Christ doesn't mean that you can relax and lazily go through life. God loves us so much that he is willing to make us uncomfortable, so that we will grow and flourish. He also loves us so much that he is willing to use us despite all our shortcomings. He is willing to equip us with the tools that we will need to be His hands and feet to reach all peoples. It is a privilege to be trusted by the Almighty God to do His work. Remember, God has a purpose for every one of us and Satan is not happy about it. We can count on trials and troubles. It's a guarantee, so we better start strengthening our armor and prepare for spiritual battle.

James 1:2-4 "Consider it pure joy, my brothers and sisters, whenever you face trials of many kinds, because you know that the testing of your faith produces perseverance. Let perseverance finish its work so that you may be mature and complete, not lacking anything."

MOMENTS OF REFLECTION:

Have you prayed specifically for forgiveness concerning any past occult involvement? I'm not talking about a general, blanket prayer saying, "Forgive me," but asking God to forgive you for reading about astrology, for going to psyhics to try and learn about the future, for seeking New Age spirit guides, etc. You want to make sure that you close all doors that Satan has been using to harass you, so that you can walk in Jesus' power of authority.

Have you allowed fear to keep the door open for Satan to harass you?

Are you actively strengthening your spiritual armor, so that you are not overcome by surprise enemy attacks on your life?

Do you need to remind yourself of who you are in Christ?

Chapter Fourteen

VICTORY ISN'T ALWAYS ABOUT WINNING

Throughout the rest of the year, I continued to attend youth group and Bible studies. I attended special youth conferences where I was able to soak in more of God together with youth from around the country. I used my talents for singing and acting to participate in church performances and local outreach events. I read my Bible regularly and I prayed to Jesus throughout the day. It was a wonderful time of spiritual growth. My faith was taking deeper root. It was transforming. I felt like I was on fire.

Of course, there were some disappointments, too. I lost several close relationships with friends and family members because they could not understand my excitement and zeal for Jesus, and His unconditional love and healing power. They did not know just how far down into the depths of despair I had gone, otherwise, they may have appreciated a little more why I was now flying so high. But then again, some people were just so uncomfortable with the idea of Jesus desiring to be personally involved in our everyday lives. They preferred to keep Him confined to Sunday morning, or to Christmas and Easter, so that they could feel like they were in control of their own lives throughout the week. It broke my heart to see a wall come up between us, but I knew that I could always pray for them. Things may have been different between us, but in my heart I would never give up on them.

Something else began brewing in my heart, too. I had planned on attending university after graduating if I could get some financial aid. I hoped to take English as my major and Theater Arts as my minor. Even though I only wanted to perform, I also didn't want to be a famously unemployed actor. I already had a childhood of hearing nothing but the struggle for money, so I was willing to be more practical. Becoming an English teacher with theater as a minor sounded like a safer, long-term option. But after seeing a performance of an international Christian theater company at my church, I began to doubt my university plans. A friend of Cody's, Evan, had joined the group for one and a half years. Evan was a wild guy who loved to drive motorcycles, but he also loved Jesus. He told me how everyone was assigned to a unit of four or five people for five months at a time. Each unit was given a geographical area to tour and to acquire bookings for the following unit. The Christian theater company performed plays on a thematic base, so that a church, school, nursing home, prison, or business could choose their own theme to highlight. The unit would learn plays on that particular theme ranging from thirty seconds to twenty-five minutes long. The group would use minimal props, so it was easy to set up anywhere. They also booked drama/communication workshops for schools and businesses that challenged people to develop stronger communication and social skills.

I had much to pray about. Cody and I were very serious about getting married in the future, so one and a half years apart might as well have been an eternity. Despite all the positive comments Evan had about the group, I also knew that nothing in this world was perfect. If I was going to honestly consider this as an alternative to my university plans, then I had to know everything – the good and the bad. I did not want to be deceived. I pressed him to tell me whatever negative aspects he saw while he was a member. The biggest thing he noticed was how there were many new or weak Christians. He saw some people struggle to live righteously. He knew some were not even Christians, but joined because it seemed like an easy way out of their current bad situation. He saw how easy it was to be consumed with learning lines, performing, acquiring new bookings and entertaining the hosts of host homes. Time for personal devotion and mediation was difficult to carve out. These were definitely some important things to ponder.

I sought the counsel of my pastor, my parents and other Christians. I spent long periods of time praying for God's wisdom and direction for my life. I did not want to do anything that I felt was not completely God's will. But the more I prayed, the more I felt compelled to go. The idea of leaving Cody for so long tore me apart, yet he encouraged me to follow my heart. And knowing that I would not necessarily have strong spiritual support during my time there puzzled me. I kept wondering if God was sending me to be an encourager to the other members more than to impact the people I would be performing for. It didn't make much sense to me, but I knew I had to go.

God even worked out the finances to pay for my airfare to Los Angeles, California and for my initial two weeks accommodation as a new recruit in training. As 1st Runner-Up to Miss Teen Canada 1985, one of my prizes was a very small scholarship for post-secondary education. The rules stipulated that the scholarship could not be used for anything else. Well, I thought I might as well try. In a letter to the pageant association, I explained what I hoped to do. Joining an international Christian theater company may not have been a school, but it had intense training in theater before and after each tour. The pageant association requested a phone interview before making their final decision. If their answer was a 'no', obtaining the money from other sources was going to be quite a challenge. I trusted if God wanted me to go that He would also provide the money.

Surprisingly, I received a letter and check in the mail awhile later. Part of me couldn't believe it. This small town girl was actually leaving for the wild city of Los Angeles. Some of my relatives thought my parents had lost their minds for allowing a nineteen year old to fly–alone–to Los Angeles. Let alone to have a total stranger pick her up and be taken into some group for one and half years. I have to admit, if it was one of my daughters, God would have to go overboard to show me it was his will. And if you knew my mother, you would know how unlike her it was to agree to such a thing. God definitely gave me, and my parents peace. And it is a good thing that God does give us His divine peace that passes all understanding when we step out in faith, because that peace carried me through my LA experience. But that's another story....

As for Cody, he promised me an engagement ring when I returned home. We became unofficially engaged. He was going to wait for me no matter what. Our hearts were sold out to each other, but we tried to give room for God to move and guide us. As a result, we spent time praying for God's will over both our lives. We asked God to bless our relationship. Although we shared our plans to marry with the Lord, we also prayed, *if* for any reason it was not His perfect will for us to be together, would He be so kind to reveal it to us while we were already physically apart. The thought of breaking up, if it was *not* God's will, while living close to each other, just seemed to be too much to handle. At the time, we had no idea how much that prayer would impact our lives forever. But that's another story....

Now that I was no longer heading off to university, I needed to earn as much money as possible before leaving for LA in January 1987. Over the summer I continued to work part-time at the shoe store. My boss did his best to give me as many extra hours as possible, but I needed more for the fall. Working weekends was not going to be enough. That began my numerous attempts for temporary employment. I worked three days telemarketing for a fundraiser. I hated it, but I would have continued working there if it wasn't for the police notice posted on the business door on my fourth day of work. The owners of the telemarketing business had ripped off the fund-raiser and did not pay any of its employees. Then I worked as a clerk for a photo development store, but it only lasted three weeks. I worked as a sales clerk for a teen's clothing store for two weeks, but the manager kept hitting on me, so I quit.

Needless to say, when I wasn't working, seeing Cody, or attending church events, I had quite a bit of free time on my hands. I decided that if I couldn't find full-time temporary employment, I would use my time wisely. I knew that the more I was full of God's word, the stronger I would be when I left for LA. That began my regime of reading the Bible five to eight hours a day until it was time to leave. I was so hungry for God's word that the hours just flew by. I understood the importance of my spiritual armor. I needed to be ready for anything.

There was just one last thing that I really wanted to do before leaving. It was time for the annual Miss London pageant. After participating in four beauty pageants over the years, I desired to enter one last time. I never expected to win because I was already scheduled to leave for LA in January, but I wanted to show the world who Julie really was – whom she had become. I was no longer hiding behind a mask. My self-confidence was no longer conjured up. I wanted to use the Miss London pageant as a platform to share what Christ had done in my life.

Not to my surprise, I made it into the top twelve finalists, which meant I was going to be part of the live telecast—just what I wanted. Now I would get my platform to share my faith. Fortunately, I hit it off well with the other girls. They all knew I was a former Miss Teen London and 1st Runner-Up to Miss Teen Canada. I heard some contestants whispering that I would be a shoe in for the title of Miss London. Then I heard others say that I was too vocal about my Christian faith, so it might hurt my chances. The head judge formerly managed Miss London's Karen Baldwin who became Miss Universe a few years earlier. He was well respected, but it was obvious that he despised me for my faith. I knew there was no chance of winning and foiling my plans for January, but that wasn't why I was there anyway. I did receive one nice surprise though. I was presented with the Talent award on pageant night.

My real victory in the pageant came when I saw the final cut of my personal interview. We were allowed to select our own location for filming, so I chose a lookout park that Cody and I had visited several times. I knew that not every question and answer was going to be included in the final cut, so I made sure to fit in as much information about my faith in every answer as possible. No matter how hard they tried to edit my interview, they just couldn't remove all the comments on my faith. I hoped and prayed that whoever watched the pageant would be encouraged to turn to Jesus and find new hope and faith in Him just as I had. It was the icing on the cake for me. I had come full circle – truly victorious.

I may have lost the pageant, but I gained so much more. No longer was I standing in the wings back stage trying to keep my wits about me, pretending that everything in my life was perfect. No longer did I need to wear a mask to cover all my shame and pain. No longer did I desperately seek my father's love and approval in order to feel valued. Christ did all of that. Christ filled my life with His perfect love. His forgiveness of my sins made everything in my life like new. I was truly reborn. I had experienced a second birth – a second chance at really living life to the fullest. The possibilities seemed endless knowing that Christ was walking with me every step of the way. I finally found significance, self- esteem and security in the only person who can freely give it – Jesus Christ.

I am not a perfect person, but I am made righteous because Jesus has forgiven me. I have purpose because God wants us all to be His voice, hands and feet to a desperate, needy, and dying world. I have peace in who I am because God says that we are all fearfully and wonderfully made. God never makes junk. He took my broken life and put me back on the potter's wheel to remold me with His wonderful healing hands. I am no longer damaged goods. My scars tell a story of how God loves us no matter what we have done.

What is your story? Do you know who Jesus Christ really is? Have you surrendered your life to Christ? Are you struggling to remain the boss of your own life? Have your past decisions created a noose around your neck?

The coolest thing of all is that Christ came to give everyone new life through His sacrifice on the cross. He didn't just come for me, so I challenge you to discover how real and awesome God truly can be in your own life – but you have to let Him in. Surrender control of your life over to the One who created you in the first place. It's the only way to have a fulfilled, purpose-driven life.

And most importantly, I challenge the youth of this generation to stand up boldly for Christ. Remember, God wants to use us no matter what our age to share His message of love and forgiveness to a lost generation. You are never too young or too old to be a soldier in Christ's army. You're life *will* be mediocre if *you choose* to be mediocre about your faith. I dare you to seek God with all your heart, with all your mind, and with all your soul with a genuine fervency. The more passionate you are about discovering who Christ is, the more He will reveal Himself to you. Then stand back, wait and watch to see what amazing things God will do in your life.

"But seek first his kingdom and his righteousness, and all these things will be given to you as well." (Matt.6:33)

As a child, I used to lie in bed holding my Sunday school bookmark. I loved how the white, felt cross glowed in the dark after absorbing light from my headboard bed lamp. But eventually the cross would fade, and I would have to turn on my lamp again. The things of this world will fade away, just like my little cross, but Jesus, the Light of the World, will never fade away. He was and is and is to come.

Matthew 24:35 "Heaven and earth with pass away, but my words will never pass away."

John 8:12 "When Jesus spoke again to the people, he said, "I am the light of the world. Whoever follows me will never walk in darkness, but will have the light of life.""

Revelation1:8 ""I am the Alpha and the Omega," says the Lord God, "who is, and who was, and who is to come, the Almighty."

MOMENTS OF REFLECTION:

If you have been a Christian for a while, can you already see the amazing difference He has made in the many areas of your life?

What kingdom are you seeking – God's or your own?

Have there been areas of darkness in your life that you are now willing to let Jesus, the light of the world, shine into?

How do you possibly see God using your story of coming to faith?

FINAL THOUGHTS

W hat do you believe? Do you know who Jesus is, and why He came, died, and rose again? What has influenced your worldview?

Josh McDowell is an amazing modern day apologist who has authored or co-authored more than 115 books. I strongly recommend anyone who desires to find answers about Christianity to read *'More Than a Carpenter'*, *'The Unshakable TRUTH'* and *''New Evidence Demands a Verdict'*. Likewise, Lee Strobel is also a well-respected apologist who has authored more than twenty books. *'The Case for a Creator'*, *'The Case for Christ'*, and *'The Case for Faith'* provide great insight from a scientific viewpoint as well as spiritual. I also recommend a documentary by Ben Stein called *'Expelled: No Intelligence Allowed'*. He interviews both creationists and evolutionists.

If you are a not a Christian, I encourage you to open your heart and mind to the message I share. Do not be afraid to ask hard questions. God can handle it. It is interesting to also mention that both Josh and Lee were professing atheists who were on a mission to prove that God did not exist. The more they searched and researched, the more the evidence proved that there had to be a God, and Christ had to be His Son. I challenge you to put aside any of your preconceived thoughts about faith and begin to look with fresh eyes at the evidence.

The Bible says, 'For God so loved the world that he gave his one and only Son, that whoever believes in him shall not perish but have eternal life. For God did not send his Son into the world to condemn the world, but to save the world through him. Whoever believes in him is not condemned, but whoever does not believe stands condemned already because they have not believed in the name of God's one and only Son. This is the verdict: **Light** has come into the world, but people loved darkness instead of **light** because their deeds were evil. Everyone who does evil hates the **light**, and will not come into the **light** for fear that their deeds will be exposed. But whoever lives by the truth comes into the **light**, so that it may be seen plainly that what they have done has been done in the sight of God.' John 3:16-21 (emphasis mine)

If you are a Christian, are you able to stand up to the world's opposing worldviews? Do you truly believe the Bible is absolute truth and relevant for today's generation? Are you passionate about getting to know your Savior more? Are you studying deeper so that you will be ready at any time to share or defend your faith? Do you really care about those who do not know Christ yet as their Savior? I challenge you to become a 'raving fan' of Jesus. Do not let past mistakes stop you from running into the forgiving arms of God. He never *ever* gives up on you and He is *always* waiting for you to return with a sincere, repentant (remorseful and regretful) heart. He is the God of second, third and fourth, etc., chances.

The Bible says, "as far as the east is from the west, so far has he removed our transgressions from us.' Psalm 103:12

Now, since going east or west has no end, that means God throws our sins away into infinity. Understand that no one can ever love you more than Christ. If you were the *only* one on earth, He would have still died for you. He has your best in mind always, even when it does not look like it. Jesus said, 'You are the **light** of the world. A town built on a hill cannot be hidden. Neither do people **light** a lamp and put it under a bowl. Instead they put it on its stand, and it gives **light** to shine before others, that they may see your good deeds and glorify your Father in heaven.' Matt.5:13-15 (emphasis mine)

The world does not need medicore, whimpy Christians. Remember how I said at the beginning that nothing can live without light? Be Christ's light in your world at school, work, social groups, neighbors, family and friends. The more you live and shine Christ's message of love, forgiveness and salvation, the more you will find significance, self-esteem and security. You will be living the best version of yourself and the most fulfilled, purpose driven life possible.

INFORMATION ON EATING DISORDERS

B ecause there are many people who are not familiar with how eating disorders affect a person, I wanted to include some basic information from NEDA (National Eating Disorders Association, nationaleatingdisorders.org). Their website holds a wealth of information on the topic. I encourage anyone to investigate their website for more in depth resources. But for my purpose, I have included information from their 'NEDA Toolkit for Parents' on 'Eating Disorder Signs, Symptoms, and Behaviors, "Common myths about eating disorders', and 'Recommended Do's and Recommended Don'ts' for parents.

ANOREXIA NERVOSA

- Dramatic weight loss
- Dresses in layers to hide weight loss
- Is preoccupied with weight , food, calories, fat grams, and dieting

- Refuses to eat certain foods, progressing to restrictions against whole categories of food (e.g., no carbohydrates, etc.)
- Makes frequent comments about feeling "fat" or overweight despite weight loss
- Complains of constipation, abdominal pain, cold intolerance, lethargy, and excess energy
- Denies feeling hungry
- Develops food rituals (e.g., eating foods in certain orders, excessive chewing, rearranging food on a plate)
- Cooks meals for others without eating
- Consistently makes excuses to avoid mealtimes or situations involving food
- Maintains an excessive, rigid exercise regimen – despite weather, fatigue, illness, or injury, the need to "burn off" calories taken in
- Withdraws from usual friends and activities and becomes more isolated, withdrawn, and secretive
- Seems concerned about eating in public
- Has limited social spontaneity
- Resists maintaining body weight at or above a minimally normal weight for age and height
- Has intense fear of weight gain or being "fat," even though underweight
- Has disturbed experience of body weight or shape, undue influence of weight or shape on self-evaluation, or denial of the seriousness of low body weight
- Postpuberty female loses menstrual period
- Feels ineffective

- Has strong need for control
- Shows inflexible thinking
- Has overly restrained initiative and emotional expression

BULIMIA NERVOSA

- In general, behaviors and attitudes indicate that weight loss, dieting, and control of food are becoming primary concerns
- Evidence of binge eating, including disappearance of large amounts of food in short periods of time or lots of empty wrappers and containers indicating consumption of large amounts of food
- Evidence of purging behaviors, including frequent trips to the bathroom after meals, signs, and/or smells of vomiting, presence of wrappers of packages of laxatives or diuretics
- Appears uncomfortable eating around others
- Develops food rituals (e.g., eats only a particular food or food group [e.g., condiments], excessive chewing, doesn't allow foods to touch)
- Skips meals or takes small potions of food at regular meals
- Steals or hoards food in strange places
- Drinks excessive amounts of water
- Uses excessive amounts of mouthwash, mints, and gum
- Hides body with baggy clothes
- Maintains excessive, rigid exercise regimen – despite weather, fatigue, illness, or injury, the need to "burn off" calories

- Shows unusual swelling of the cheeks or jaw area
- Has calluses on the back of the hands and knuckles from self-induced vomiting
- Teeth are discolored, stained
- Creates lifestyle schedule or rituals to make time for binge-and-purge sessions
- Withdraws from usual friends and activities
- Looks bloated from fluid retention
- Frequently diets
- Shows extreme concern with body weight and shape
- Has secret recurring episodes of binge eating (eating in a discrete period of time an amount of food that is much larger than most individuals would eat under similar circumstances); feels lack of control over ability to stop eating
- Purges after a binge (e.g., self-induced vomiting, abuse of laxatives, diet pills and/or diuretics, excessive exercise, fasting)
- Body weight is typically within the normal weight range; maybe be overweight

BINGE EATING DISORDER (COMPULSIVE EATING DISORDER)

- Evidence of binge eating, including disappearance of large amounts of food in short periods of time or lots of empty wrappers and containers indicating consumption of large amounts of food

- Develops food rituals (e.g., eats only a particular food or food group [e.g., condiments], excessive chewing, doesn't allow foods to touch)
- Steals or hoards food in strange places
- Hides body with baggy clothes
- Creates lifestyle schedule or rituals to make time for binge-sessions
- Skips meals or takes small portions of food at regular meals
- Has periods of uncontrolled, impulsive, or continuous eating beyond the point of feeling comfortably full
- Does not purge
- Engages in sporadic fasting or repetitive dieting
- Body weight varies from normal to mild, moderate, or severe obesity

OTHER EATING DISORDERS

- Any combination of the above

NEDA TOOLKIT for Parents
Common myths about eating disorders

This information is intended to help dispel all-too-common misunderstandings about eating disorders and those affected by them. If your family member has an eating disorder, you may wish to share this information with others (i.e., other family member, friends, teachers, coaches, family physician).

Eating disorders are not an illness

Eating disorders are a complex medical/psychiatric illness. Eating disorders are classified as a mental illness in the American Psychiatric Association's *Diagnostic and Statistical Manual of Mental Health Disorders (DSM-IV)*, are considered to often have a biologic basis, and co-occur with other mental illness such as major depression, anxiety, or obsessive-complusive disorder.

Eating disorders are uncommon

They are common. Anorexia nervosa, bulimia nervosa, and binge-eating disorder are on the rise in the United States and worldwide. Among U.S. females in their teens and 20s, the prevalence of clinical and subclinical anorexia may be as high as 15%. Anorexia nervosa ranks as the 3rd most common chronic illness among adolescent U.S. females. Recent studies suggest that up to 7% of U.S. females have had bulimia. Current findings suggest that binge-eating disorder affects 0.7% to 4% of the general population.

Eating disorders are a choice

People do not choose to have eating disorders. They develop over time and require appropriate treatment to address the complex medical/psychiatric symptoms and underlying issues.

Eating disorders occur only in females

Eating disorders occur in males. Few solid statistics are available on the prevalence of eating disorders in males, but the disorders are believed to be more common than currently reflected in statistics because of under-diagnosis. An estimated one-fourth of anorexia diagnoses in children are in males. The National Collegiate Athletic Association carried out studies on the incidence of eating-disordered behavior among athletes in the 1990s, and reported that of those athletes who reported having an eating disorder, 7% were male. For binge-eating disorder, preliminary research suggests equal prevalence among males and females. Incidence in males may be underreported because females are more likely to seek help, and health practitioners are more likely to consider an eating disorder diagnosis in females. Differences in symptoms exist between males and females: females are more likely to focus on weight loss; males are more likely to focus on muscle mass. Although issues such as altering diet to increase muscle mass, over-exercise, or steroid misuse are not yet criteria for eating disorders, a growing body of research indicates that these factors are associated with many, but not all, males with eating disorders.

Men who suffer from eating disorders tend to be gay

Sexual preference has no correlation with developing an eating disorder.

Anorexia nervosa is the only serious eating disorder

All eating disorders can have damaging physical and psychological consequences. Although excess weight loss is a feature of anorexia nervosa, effects of other eating disorders can also be serious or life threatening, such as the electrolyte imbalance associated with purging.

A person cannot die from bulimia

While the rate of death from bulimia nervosa is much lower than that seen with anorexia nervosa, a person with bulimia can be at high risk for death and sudden death because of purging and its impact on the heart and electrolyte imbalances. Laxatives use and excessive exercise can increase risk of death in individuals who are actively bulimic.

Subclinical eating disorders are not serious

Although a person may not fulfill the diagnostic criteria for an eating disorder, the consequences associated with disordered eating (e.g., frequent vomiting, excessive exercise, anxiety) can have long-term consequences and requires intervention. Early intervention may also prevent progression to a full-blown clinical eating disorder.

NEDA TOOLKIT for Parents
How to be supportive Recommended Do's

- Educate yourself on eating disorders; learn the jargon
- Learn the differences between facts and myths about weight, nutrition, and exercise
- Ask what you can do to help
- Listen openly and reflectively
- Be patient and nonjudgmental
- Talk with the person in a kind way when you are calm and not angry, frustrated, or upset
- Have compassion when the person brings up painful issues about underlying problems
- Let him/her know you only want the bet for him/her
- Remind the person that he/she has people who care and support him/her
- Suggest professional help in a gentle way
- Offer to go along
- Be flexible and open with your support
- Be honest
- Compliment the person's personality, successes, and accomplishments
- Encourage all activities suggested by the treating care team, such as keeping appointments and medication compliance
- Encourage social activities that don't involve food
- Encourage the person to buy foods that he/she will want to eat (as opposed to only "healthy" foods)
- Help the person to be patient

- Help with the person's household chores (e.g., laundry, cleaning) as needed
- Remember: recovery takes time and food may always be a difficult issue
- Remember: recovery work is up to the affected person
- Show care, concern, and understanding
- Ask how he/she is feeling
- Try to be a good role model
- Understand that the person is not looking for attention or pity

Recommended Don'ts

- Accuse or cause feelings of guilt
- Invade privacy and contact the patient's doctors or others to check up behind his/her back
- Demand weight changes (even if clinically necessary for health)
- Insist the person eat every type of food at the table
- Invite the person out for social occasions where the main focus is food
- Invite the person to go clothes shopping
- Making eating, food, clothes, or appearance the focus of conversation
- Make promises or rules you cannot or will not follow (e.g., promising not to tell anyone)
- Threaten (e.g., if you do this once more I'll…)
- Offer more help than you are qualified to give
- Create guilt or place blame on the person

- Put timetables on recovery
- Take the person's actions personally
- Try to change the person's attitudes about eating or nag about food
- Try to control the person's life
- Use scare tactics to get the person into treatment, but do call 911 if you believe the person's condition is life-threatening

My eating disorders definitely fueled my depression. Webmed.com discusses the connection between eating disorders and depression.

Eating Disorders and Depression

By Peter Jaret
WebMD Feature
Reviewed by Brunilda Nazario, MD

WebMD Archive

Eating disorders often begin with the best of intentions – a desire to lose weight and control eating. But in some people, those good intentions go badly wrong, resulting in anorexia nervosa, bulimia, binge eating, or other disorders.

Why some people are a risk for eating disorders isn't clear. But surveys show that depression is often a factor. In a 2008 study by researchers at the University of Pittsburgh Medical Center, for example, 24% of bipolar patients met the criteria for eating disorders. An estimated 44% had trouble controlling their eating.

As many as half of all patients diagnosed with binge eating disorder have a history of depression, according to the National Institute of Diabetes and Digestive and Kidney Diseases. Binge eating afflicts 3% of adults in the U.S., making it the most common eating disorder.

Depression also plagues many people with anorexia, another common eating disorder. People with anorexia fail to eat enough food to maintain a healthy weight. The results can be tragic. Studies show that anorexics are 50 times more likely than the general population to die as a result of suicide.

The Link Between Depression and Eating Disorders

Depression may lead to eating disorders, but there's also evidence that eating disorders can result in depression. "Being severely underweight and malnourished, which is common in anorexia, can cause physiological changes that are know to negatively affect mood states," says Lisa Lilenfel, PhD, an associate professor of clinical psychology at Argosy University in Arlington, Va., who specializes in eating disorders.

Depression in people with eating disorders typically has its own unique features, according to Ira M. Sacker, MD, an eating disorders specialist at Langone Medical Center at New York University and author of *Regaining Your Self: Understanding and Conquering the Eating Disorder Identity.*

"People who develop eating disorders feel as people that they're not good enough," Sacker says. "They become obsessed with perfectionism. That perfectionism begins to focus on what they eat. But underlying it is depression and anxiety. Often, these patients have suffered a lot of emotional trauma."

People with binge eating disorder are frequently overweight or obese, for instance. This can lead them to feel chronically depressed about the way they look. After succumbing to an episode of binge eating, they may feel disgusted with themselves, worsening their depression.

PULL QUOTES

ICE CREAM, lyrics by Herron Campbell, from Anne of Green Gables, The Musical

'Stairway to Heaven' song by Led Zeppelin, 1971

"More than a Carpenter" by Josh McDowell, Tyndale House Publishers, Inc., 2011

taken from McDowell's "Evidence That Demands a Verdict", vol.1, 1972 pgs. 40-48, Thomas Nelson Publishers, 1992

taken from knowwhatyoubelieve.com

"Case for a Creator" by Lee Strobel, Zondervan Publishers, 2004

"Teahouse of the August Moon" play by John Patrick and Vern Sneider, 1953

"The Miracle Worker" play by William Gibson, 1957

Thomas A. Edison, U.S. inventor, (1847-1931), quotation-spage.com

"The Lesson" play by Eugene Ionesco, 1951

"The Matchmaker" play by John B. Keane and Thornton Wilder, the non-musical version of "Hello Dolly", 1957

"I Remember Mama" play by John Van Druten, 1944, based on Kathryn Forbes' novel, "Mama's Bank Account"

"I Hate Men" song by Cole Porter from the musical "Kiss Me Kate" written by Samuel and Bella Spewack, 1948

Roman soldier "caligae" sandals, information found on tribune-sandtriumphs.org

Roman soldier "scutum" (shield), information found under "Scutum (shield) on en.m.wikipedia.org

Information taken from NEDA (National Eating Disorders Association, nationaleatingdisorders.org)

Information taken from Webmed.com on Eating Disorders and Depression, by Peter Jaret

ABOUT THE AUTHOR

After Julie competed in the Miss London 1987 pageant, she traveled for 1½ years in the United States and Canada with an international Christian Theater company. While on the road, she performed in churches, schools, prisons, nursing homes, etc. doing plays on a thematic base. She also conducted drama/communication workshops for all ages.

During her time in the theater company, she met and married her husband, Tore Stautland, from Norway. They took a week off the road from their Indiana touring area to drive up and get married in London, Ontario on September 25th, 1987.

Julie brought Tore back to Canada where he obtained Canadian status. After establishing work, together they volunteered as youth leaders for nine years at their church. Julie led worship for 4 years, and worked with Tore on the mission committee and church productions.

At, 21, Julie also had to have bone spurs removed from both heels which she developed when taking tap dancing lessons. The procedure involved breaking both her ankles, so she had to learn how to walk all over again.

Julie volunteered for Compassion Canada at numerous concert events and tours while Tore was the Artist Relations Director for 5 years.

At the same time, Julie was an itinerant speaker in schools, churches and conferences. She told her life story in schools on the theme of 'making positive choices'. In churches, she spoke of how courageous Christian youth shared the love of Jesus that saved her from the brink of suicide. At conferences, she spoke on recovering for eating disorders and sexual abuse.

Tore and Julie also housed a few college age students for four years. Julie has affectionately commented that this experience helped prepare her for parenthood.

Julie studied up to grade 10 in classical voice while Tore took on a contract at CWR publishing in England for one year as VP of International Distribution.

For two years they ran "Christian Expo" in Toronto, an event where various Christian ministries and businesses could reach the public.

During Julie's speaking years, she began to develop environmental allergies towards pollution and many chemicals. Her weakened immune system triggered 15 years of chronic daily common migraines, chronic sinusitis, fibromyalgia, and interstitial cystitis (I.C. bladder syndrome). As well, she suffered many years with digestive issues. On top of that, the incorrect curve in her neck, either from birth, or from various accidents, triggered classic migraines.

Therefore, when Julie became pregnant with their first child, Mercedes, she tried to stop taking her antihistamines. But after three rounds of antibiotics for sinus infections in her first trimester, she was forced to take antihistamines throughout both her pregnancies. Thankfully, God protected their children from any harm. Mercedes was born in 1999, and Trinity was born in 2001.

Julie ceased speaking and became a full-time mother and homeschool teacher. Tore started their media company, Trillennium Media Group Inc. (TMG INC.) Besides selling air-time for four stations, TMG produces TV shows, infomercials, films, documentaries, etc. TMG currently produces '700 Club Canada' and 'The Jim Cantelon Show".

Julie's health continued to deteriorate when the girls were little. The medical community could offer nothing more for her. Julie had already changed her diet, detoxed, took a laundry list of supplements, replaced chemical products with natural ones, but it was not enough. She became desperate for relief from the constant pain, so that she could be involved in her girls' lives instead of always lying down and taking pills. By accident, she discovered that her pain and symptoms less-ened while on a two week trip to Florida. Subsequent trips to Florida continued to show improvement. This began their pattern of visiting Florida off and on throughout the year for her health. The girls continue school through homeschooling. Today Julie is off of all daily drugs and her symptoms have decreased significantly.

Julie enjoys seeing her young pilot, Mercedes fly, and her young artist/songwriter, Trinity create, as well as watching them both participate in fencing and archery.

As the girls are nearing adulthood, Julie is looking forward to being more involved in TV, other media forms, and speaking again.

Tore, Julie and the girls currently reside in the Niagara region.

PICTURES

3 months old

1st day of grade one for me

9 years old at piano lessons

My beloved piano teacher

1st place at the science fair

One of my public speaking awards

My role as Diana Barry in "Anne of Green Gables"

On my left is my favorite teacher, 'Miss Wallace'/'Mrs. Millcroft'

My role as Becky Thatcher in "Tom Sawyer"

My Dad and his Dodge

15 years old and still quite thin

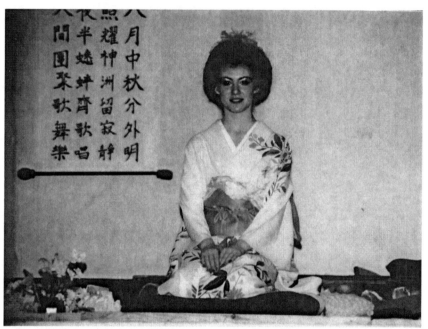

My role as Lotus Blossom in "Teahouse of the August Moon"

Turkey Festival queen contestants

CONTESTANTS FOR THE title of Miss Turkey Festival Queen 1983 assembled for a luncheon last Wednesday at the Pine Ridge Restaurant in Strathroy. They are, in the first row, from left to right, Denise Kirk, 14, of Mt. Brydges, Lisa LeBritton, 17, of Strathroy, and Julie vander Maden, 15, of Strathroy. In the back row are from left to right, Carman Van Heeswyk, 15, of Kerwood, Shari Gordyn, 15, of Kerwood, Jane Ross, 17, of Strathroy, Teresa Thuss, 16, of Strathroy, and Cay Chazalon, 15, of Strathroy.

(Staff)

Queen makes draw

STRATHROY TURKEY FESTIVAL Queen Julie Vander-Maden drew one of the winning tickets in the art draw held at the third annual art show held by the Strathroy Art group on July 1. Above, Julie, left, is seen with art group president Dot McAteer. Mayor Thomas Wolder drew the other winning ticket. The art show was held in the Olde Fire Hall gallery at the rear of the town hall.

Queen has part in Huron production

Strathroy's Turkey Festival Queen, 15-year-old Julie VanderMaden, has been awarded a part in "The Helen Keller Story", playing at the Huron Country Playhouse from July 19-30.

The SDCI Theatre Arts student, who hopes to make the stage her career, auditioned for the role of one of six blind girls who appear in one scene at the beginning of the play. Julie has been rehearsing at the Grand Bend Theatre and says she is finding the experience very worthwhile.

"The experience is great. I'm noticing a lot of things that the professionals do," said Julie last week.

Crowned 1983 Strathroy Turkey Festival Queen at the festival

Performing duties as the Turkey Festival Queen

My actor photo for the Huron County Playhouse

My introduction to Prime Minister Pierre Elliot Trudeau

Performing duties at the Royal Winter Fair as the
Strathroy Turkey Festival Queen

Hair modeling for a salon

25lbs heavier at Christmas time

At the Miss Teen London 1984 pageant

"La Leçon" French play, role as 'The Student"

"No Business Like Show Business" Variety Show

"No Business Like Show Business" Variety Show

"The Matchmaker" London Community Theatre

Miss Teen London 1985 pageant night

Miss Teen London 1985

MAYOR WOLDER PRESENTING
JULIE VANDERMADEN WITH
AN HONOURARY CITIZEN'S
CERTIFICATE ON FEB.18/85.

Honorary Citizen of Strathroy award

Miss Teen Canada 1985 cover of program

TAMARA LAMB
Miss Teen Duncan

CORINA TAYLOR
Miss Teen Victoria

ALLYSON PHELAN
Miss Teen Vancouver

COLLEEN BELL
Miss Teen Prince George

TYMMARAH ZEHR
Miss Teen Grande Cache

TERRI STEVENS
Miss Teen Saskatoon

LORETTA BAERG
Miss Teen Prince Albert

LEANNE HALL
Miss Teen Regina

KIMBERLEY BOISVENUE
Miss Teen Yorkton

VALERIE CHUDY
Miss Teen Flin Flon

miss teen canada pageant 1985

SUSAN CUNNINGHAM
Miss Teen Georgian Bay

JILLIAN HENNESSY
Miss Teen Kitchener/Waterloo

TRACY STEELE
Miss Teen Brantford

CLAUDELLE DUGUAY
Miss Teen Hamilton

LYNN SARACHMAN
Miss Teen Burlington

CHANTAL MORASSE
Miss Teen Montreal

SYLVIE JOBIN
Miss Teen Trois Rivières

DENISE LEVESQUE
Miss Teen Quebec City

SUSAN SMITH
Miss Teen Hartland

TANYA MILTON
Miss Teen Saint John

Miss Teen Canada 1985 contestants

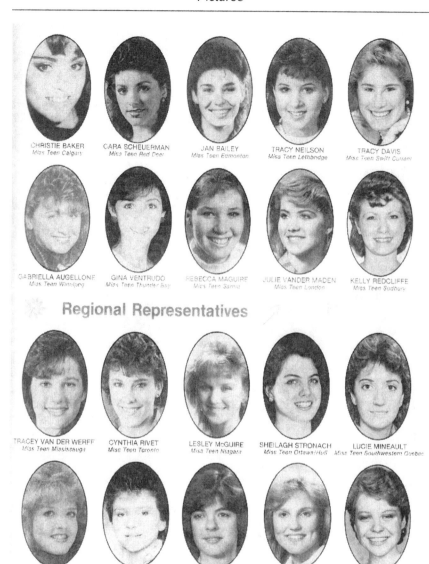

CHRISTIE BAKER
Miss Teen Calgary

CARA SCHEUERMAN
Miss Teen Red Deer

JAN BAILEY
Miss Teen Edmonton

TRACY NEILSON
Miss Teen Lethbridge

TRACY DAVIS
Miss Teen Swift Current

GABRIELLA AUGELLONE
Miss Teen Winnipeg

GINA VENTRUDO
Miss Teen Thunder Bay

REBECCA MAGUIRE
Miss Teen Sarnia

JULIE VANDER MADEN
Miss Teen London

KELLY REDCLIFFE
Miss Teen Sudbury

Regional Representatives

TRACEY VAN DER WERFF
Miss Teen Mississauga

CYNTHIA RIVET
Miss Teen Toronto

LESLEY McGUIRE
Miss Teen Niagara

SHEILAGH STRONACH
Miss Teen Ottawa/Hull

LUCIE MINEAULT
Miss Teen Southwestern Quebec

CINDY MacCALLUM
Miss Teen Riverview

TERRI LYNN SMITH
Miss Teen Halifax/Dartmouth

LISA DECKER
Miss Teen Cape Breton

LISA KUJBIDA
Miss Teen P.E.I.

NADINE WHALEN
Miss Teen Newfoundland

Miss Teen Canada 1985 contestants

1st Runner-Up to Miss Teen Canada 1985 pageant night

Modeling

Strathroy Turkey Festival Parade as Miss Teen London 1985

Modeling

My 1977 Buick Skyhawk

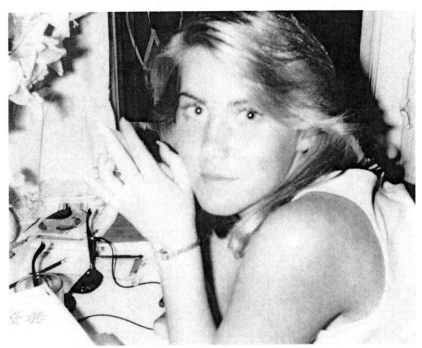

This picture was taken by the guy I dated who was suicidal like myself.

The evening I crowned the next Miss Teen London 1986

Received the Talent Award at the Miss London 1987 pageant

Performing at the Miss London 1987 pageant

Doing the pageant walk at Miss London 1987 pageant

My beautiful family today

CPSIA information can be obtained at www.ICGtesting.com
Printed in the USA
LVOW07s0237230916

505664LV00003B/1/P